THE SOUTH STRIKES BACK

THE SOUTH
STRIKES BACK

Hodding Carter III

NEGRO UNIVERSITIES PRESS
WESTPORT, CONNECTICUT

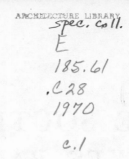

To My Father,

for obvious reasons.

CONTENTS

CONTENTS

THE SOUTH STRIKES BACK

CHAPTER I

Background for Resistance

I think that since the Supreme Court decision segregation has become inevitable. The integrationists have aroused folks as they might never have been aroused otherwise. Through the 40s and early 50s most Southerners were apathetic, resigned to what they felt was inevitable. By raising an immediate target, the integrationists hurt themselves. In fact, I think the stupidest thing that was done was the wholesale onslaught by the integrationists on the whole area at one time . . . By insisting on immediate integration everywhere, they sent a whole region up in arms. They should have nibbled slowly at the edges.

William Simmons, Editor, *The Citizens' Council*

THE DECADE from the conclusion of World War II to the Supreme Court desegregation decision of 1954 was in

many ways a halcyon period for the exponents of gradu-
alism in the handling of the South's racial problems. The
mass of white Southerners were opposed to any major,
drastic change in the status of the Negro, as historically
they had ever been; but there was nevertheless a growing
measure of tolerance of those who sought to eliminate the
more blatant forms of discrimination. This toleration existed only so long as the goals remained within the framework of segregation, but it was tolerance nonetheless.
Perceptible throughout the South was a widening acceptance, in theory at least, of the concept that the "separate
but equal" doctrine which had long been the region's
racial byword should be applied as strenuously toward
providing equal facilities and opportunities as toward in-
suring that those facilities and opportunities should be
separate.

This decade witnessed the eclipse, through death or
retirement or defeat, of such notorious demagogues as
Senator Theodore G. Bilbo and Congressman John Rankin, both of Mississippi, and Gene Talmadge of Georgia.
While their political places were often taken by equally
ardent defenders of segregation, the nation's attention began shifting more and more to the men who fell under
the loose classification of "Southern liberal," a term which,
while it took in many who were far more Southern than
liberal, did include some whose starting point on all racial
matters was 180 degrees to the left of the South's gaudier
former champions. Most, if not all, of these men were not
politicians, but many of them reached further with their
pens than the politicians had with their words.

It was during this decade also that the federal courts began the slow but thorough cutting away of many of the South's—and the nation's—Jim Crow laws governing in interstate travel, public housing, public transportation, and higher education. Each new ruling received the usual denunciation reserved for such "outside interference"; but with no effective organized opposition each was grudgingly accepted. It was an increasingly common event for the white Southerner to discover that a Negro was attending his state university's graduate school or that Negroes were ordering meals in the white sections of railroad dining cars even south of Atlanta. Overt violence in such cases was exceedingly rare.

Increasingly also, the casual visitor to the South would hear from his hosts such pronouncements as, "Segregation will never end in my lifetime, of course, but my children will see its end"; or "I know that segregation is morally wrong, but I was brought up believing in it. Maybe my kids won't be as prejudiced." This was a new climate for the South, a mixture of passivity and troubled conscience, of acceptance of some changes and resignation to others, but it was one that many believed was growing stronger with each year.

More indications of this appeared than mere generalized expressions by isolated individuals. Tentative biracial groups were putting out more and more exploratory feelers each year, groping toward increased communication and understanding between the hitherto isolated islands of the white and colored community. State after Southern state outlawed the masked activities of the Ku

Klux Klan as a seemingly final result of regional disenchantment with an organization which in the South of Reconstruction had been the symbol of its finest ideals. When other, often more vicious, hate organizations such as the Columbians multiplied immediately after the war, they were summarily broken by the massed opposition of Southern whites and their state governments. The "New South" was becoming something more than had been envisioned in the shadow of the post-Reconstruction period when Georgia's eloquent Henry W. Grady had implanted the hopeful phrase in the minds of Yankee and onetime Rebel alike.

This was hardly the entire picture, however, nor was it the only one. The mores of an area do not die so suddenly as to be placed in any such rigid category or perspective by a contemporary chronicler. Enough resentment existed over the changes that were taking place or being attempted, no matter how gradually or minutely, to create a receptive climate for the abortive third-party movement of 1948. Four Southern states backed the presidential ticket of the States' Rights party, the "Dixiecrats," four states which left the confines of a party allegiance older than segregation itself. Defeat, foreordained or not, did not diminish either that resentment nor the collective wish for a suitable outlet for it.

Equalization of facilities, particularly in the public schools, was in most areas more a matter of intent than reality. It was with great reluctance that a Southern state legislature would allocate funds on anywhere near a 50–50 basis to white and Negro schools, the proportion more commonly being two or four to one in favor of the white schools. The four years prior to the Supreme Court's desegregation decision saw a trend toward equality in allocations; but it was a trend prodded by the threat of just such a court action.

Rarely in the Deep South, as always, was a Negro's murderer, if he was white, found guilty by his peers; and if he was convicted, the death penalty was even more rarely pronounced, no matter what the circumstances. On the other hand, crimes of black against white still met a swift and sure retribution. Lynch law, once a common phenomenon, was no longer practiced or condoned by the mass of Southern whites as it had once been, but there were still Negroes who found that the doors of their jails were conveniently open when the mob came.

Activist Negro groups, and especially the National Association for the Advancement of Colored People—the Negro organization most hated and feared by the Southern white—were certainly not willing to concede that much had been granted the Southern Negro. Progress within the confines of segregation was, by and large, no progress as far as they were concerned. In fact, the targets for the publicists and the orators of the NAACP were increasingly the "Southern liberals," since, rightly or wrongly, that organization felt that these more sophisticated proponents of change within the pattern of segregation were the biggest obstacles to its eventual destruction. To those who wanted an immediate end to segregation, the Southern liberals were, as Lillian Smith named them, the "killers of the dream" of equality.

Such, then, was the South upon which the Supreme Court decision of May 1954 exploded, a region slowly groping its way out of the racial pattern of centuries, not fast enough for some, too fast for others. There was no immediate Southern public reaction to the decision save that of dazed stillness, no uniformity of comment from the politicians or the newspapers of the South. Some indulged in angry protests, others in calls for "study," others took refuge in "no comment." As in the aftermath of a war's first engagement, there followed a period of hurried regrouping and hesitant probing of the enemy's intentions.

Strangely enough, the one group which might best have used this temporary lull was the most inactive, the most silent body of all. The minority of the South's population which had anticipated the Court's decision included few of the leading Southern liberals. This was apparently true despite the fact that many of these same men and women had for years attacked the immorality of the South's position and its untenability in the face of a democratic society's demands. Suddenly, when a need arose for some kind of middle-ground action, there was none. "Acceptance" and "calm"; these were the two words heard most often from this group, but action was rapidly becoming the order of the day. For some reason there had been no planning by the middle of the roaders, but the activists on both right and left either already had, or soon did have, their plan of action.

Certainly calm was the one element least likely to prevail after the initial shock. The potential end of segregation in the schools meant to most white Southerners the beginning of integration in every aspect of life, social as well as academic. To argue otherwise was to argue alone. On this subject there was general agreement. This feeling was not made any less intense when the NAACP's spokesmen announced that it proposed to press for the immediate implementation of the Court's decision throughout the entire South. This announcement, coupled with the NAACP's subsequent court actions and public pronouncements, united the entire white South as it had not been united since the Civil War.

This coming together was and is as real as it is unrealistic, combining as it does such diverse states as Virginia and Mississippi, as Texas and South Carolina, Alabama and Florida. But under the stress of a similar emotion such a unity had been established once before. As far as many white Southerners were concerned, the war had begun again, and the blanket salvos of the "outsiders" were reason enough for togetherness.

The pressure for unity came from outside the South. The precedent for it came from history. But the cement to hold it together once the first flaring of passion had subsided came from within. Lacking this cement, the Southern states might have gone their separate ways, each accommodating itself to the Court's demands as best its citizens and leadership would allow. With this hardening element, however, almost the entire region was joined within the space of little more than a year in "massive resistance" to any integration whatsoever. The catalyst was supplied by a grass-roots organization of Southern whites which named itself the Citizens' Council.

From a tiny nucleus of men in the Yazoo-Mississippi Delta in the summer of 1954, the Citizens' Council expanded into an area-wide apparatus claiming some 300,000 members. From the single sheet throwaways of a duplicating machine its propaganda effort expanded to include a newspaper, a regional television and radio show, and an army of speakers for any occasion from a school assembly to a Rotarians' luncheon. Belying its "non-political" beginning, its membership spread to include the legislative leaders and the legislative followers, the gubernatorial hopefuls and the governors, the senators and the mayors, of countless Southern states and towns. The strength of each state's organization varied from Florida's 8000-member Council to Mississippi and Alabama's 80,000 plus, but in every state it made itself known.

With the rise of the Citizens' Councils came the decline of the Southern liberal (or moderate, as the term evolved). The tenderly nurtured bi-racial commissions dried up in the heat of local hatred or suspicion. The moderate became first an isolated figure, then more and more the subject of comprehensive efforts to silence him. Just as in any area at war, the white South's majority had no need or respect or tolerance for neighbors who did not believe wholeheartedly in its efforts. Those who spoke out in opposition were pasted with the labels of "traitor" and "nest-fouler," "Red" and "nigger lover" and coveter of "Yankee dollars." The device was greatly effective.

Throughout the South, state legislatures erected a hodge-podge of stopgap legal barriers to integration. Throughout the South the NAACP found itself under steadily increasing pressures, its membership declining or going underground, its name becoming a synonym for the enemy. Throughout the South the Supreme Court, scarcely less than the NAACP, was attacked as "Communist infiltrated," criminal, or insane, its rulings labeled "unenforceable" or "laughable." The century's great crusade became in much of the white South the crusade for segregation and states' rights, and at its head or nearby moved in nearly every state the Citizens' Councils.

Too much credit or blame should not be given to any organization, especially a loosely knit one, for the mobilization of a region for concerted action. And the analysis by a native of his region's actions may be suspect, perspective being often dimmed by too close proximity. Nevertheless, the fact remains that in the South the Citizens' Council takes and merits most of the credit for whatever success massive resistance, with all its implications, has had; and there is little or no disposition by anyone, politician or not, to argue the point. Certainly this assumption of responsibility is valid in Mississippi; and it is with Mississippi's progenitive Citizens' Councils that the remainder of this study is concerned.

Such a drastic narrowing of the subject matter may be objected to on a number of grounds. But there are other factors which favor an especial examination of Mississippi's Councils. The first, which contains something of a contradiction, is that the story of the Mississippi phenomenon contains elements of an examination of the entire region. This is true because the movement was begun in Mississippi, was spread from Mississippi by Mississippians, and is still controlled to significant extent from Mississippi.

The second factor is that Mississippi's Citizens' Council presents the important features of the Councils of each of the other Southern states, but in far stronger form than any other state organization can boast. It is at once the biggest, the most tightly organized, and the most powerful Citizens' Council of them all.

The third and last factor favoring such a localized study is that Mississippi itself, as a state, is a classic representative of the Deep South. In tradition, in tribulation, in present activity, in ambition, and in future possibilities, Mississippi *is* the Deep South, and the presence and activity of the Citizens' Councils within such an environment can be interpreted in more general terms than those simply of Mississippi.

CHAPTER II

The Councils Form

This is no time to be calm. We have been as docile
and calm as the Asinus while our head is being thrust into
the yoke. If in one mighty voice we do not protest this
travesty on justice, we might as well surrender. The Supreme Court awaits our reaction. Be deliberate, yes, but
not calm. Be determined, yes, but not impulsive. Be res-
olute, yes, but not violent.

Judge Tom P. Brady, *Black Monday*

THE SUPREME COURT school decision of May 17, 1954,
declaring racial segregation unconstitutional in public
schools, did not come as a surprise to the political leaders
of Mississippi, no matter how it may have affected the
mass of the state's citizens. In the year prior to the decision the state legislature had taken several definite steps

either to influence the Court's decision or to circumvent any ruling unfavorable to the continuation of racial segregation in the public school system. The first such action had come in a special session of the legislature in November–December 1953, when an "equalization" program for the public schools was enacted calling for equal salaries for white and Negro teachers, and equal transportation, equal buildings, and equal school opportunities for all the state's children, white or black. The program was not to go into effect, however, until after the anticipated Supreme Court decision was handed down and unless it was favorable to the state's position on continued separation of the races. There were neither to be funds allotted nor bonds issued for the program unless such a "favorable" decision was given.

Later, in the legislature's regular session in early 1954, the lawmakers came up with additional safeguards against what was anticipated by many to be an inevitably unfavorable decision by the Court. First, rather than provide enough funds for the public schools to operate for a full two years, the legislature appropriated only enough money for the 1954–55 school session. The representatives reasoned that they would have to be called into session again after the decision to provide the estimated 18 million dollars which would be needed for the schools' operations in 1955–56, and that at such a time a program could be worked out to meet any problems created by the Supreme Court decision. They apparently decided that this was the only sure way to insure their being reconvened before the next regular session in 1956.

As a second and equally important step during the 1954 regular session, the legislature established the Legal Education Advisory Committee. This committee would, the bill said:

> . . . formulate a plan or plans of legislation, prepare drafts of suggested laws, and recommend course of action for consideration whereby the state may, by taxation or otherwise, provide education and/or assistance in obtaining education for all its citizens consistent with the provisions of the constitution of the United States and constitution of the state of Mississippi.

This bill was offered to the legislature by Speaker of the House Walter Sillers, one of the most powerful politicians of the state and later, whether or not a member, a chief spokesman for the Citizens' Councils in the House. The LEAC was established, the bill continued, since "in order to preserve and promote the best interest of both races and the public welfare, it is necessary to maintain separate education and separate schools for the white and colored races."

Before the legislature adjourned it passed one other important bill, this one placing a constitutional amendment before the people in November 1954. The amendment was designed to tighten voting qualifications, and it passed without much opposition. The legislature then adjourned, and Mississippi awaited the Court's ruling.

Mississippi was a state which had traditionally held strongly to both the theory and practice of segregation, and in which ramifications of that practice had reached

23

into almost every aspect of life. With the highest proportion of Negroes to white of any state—some 45.4 in the 1950 census—and the lowest number of Negro voters in any Southern state—22,000 in the 1952 presidential election—the patterns of racial segregation seemed as secure in 1954 as they had in 1900. Only a year or so before 1954 had the "separate but equal" clause in the state constitution even begun to be seriously applied. In the 1952–53 school year, the state had spent four times as much on transporting whites to school as Negroes, and three times as much on white instruction. And Mississippi was a state whose mores were as well represented in Congress in the present as they had been in the past by such men as Senators Bilbo and Vardaman and Representative John Rankin. The state's senior senator, James O. Eastland, was to be re-elected in the summer of 1954 in a campaign marked by the two chief contenders scrambling to claim Bilbo's mantle as their own.

Nevertheless, some observers had noted a change in attitudes of many Mississippians in the years after World War II. Though not criticizing segregation itself, some newspapers had attacked politicians for taking extreme positions on racial issues, and in some communities genuine efforts had been made to bring the Negro public facilities up to par with the white. Equalization was beyond the talking state at any rate, as noted, and considerable public opinion, as represented in legislative action, had been mobilized behind the idea prior to the Supreme Court decision.

It was upon this state and this state of mind that the Supreme Court decision of May 17, 1954, was imposed. The actual wording of the decision is unimportant here, but the effect it had of placing the doctrine of "separate but equal" school systems outside the pale of constitutionality is of great importance. A Southern Regional Council report summed up Mississippi's public reaction with the statement that "Mississippi officials are unanimous in their reaction: the Court decision will not be accepted." The Jackson *Clarion-Ledger* carried an editorial which said that "May 17, 1954, may be recorded as a black day of tragedy for the South . . ." The Jackson *Daily News's* lead editorial was entitled "Blood on the Marble Steps." There were less violent reactions, however. The Greenville *Delta Democrat-Times* of May 20, 1954, noted the "Delta's calm acceptance of the decision" and said that the Delta's Congressman Smith had "urged calm consideration . . . of how the ruling will ultimately affect Mississippi . . ."

On May 23, the National Association for the Advancement of Colored People was reported to be seeking the immediate end of segregated schools everywhere. On the following day, the late Walter White, then executive secretary of the NAACP, was quoted in a United Press story as saying that "we think it is about time the guarantees of the Emancipation Proclamation, the 14th and 15th Amendments, should be implemented. The South is more ready for change from segregation to integration than the professional politicians believe it to be. . . ."

The "professional politicians" indeed did not believe the

state was ready, and they soon presented a united front in telling the world so. On May 27, 1954, Senator Eastland declared that the Court had shown a "disregard of its oath and duty" in handing down its ruling. On the floor of Congress, United States Representative John Bell Williams described May 17 as "Black Monday," a phrase which although hardly original with the representative was to stick as a Southern epithet.

It was in this atmosphere that Judge Tom P. Brady, a circuit judge of Brookhaven, Mississippi, gave in late May a speech entitled "Black Monday" to a meeting of the Sons of the American Revolution in Greenwood, Mississippi. The talk was chiefly concerned with the errors involved in the Supreme Court decision, according to the judge, the most important being that it involved a reversal of a half century of legal precedent and that it did not take into account the Negro's basic inferiority to the white race. Judge Brady, a native Mississippian and graduate of Lawrenceville, Yale, and the University of Mississippi Law School, was apparently talking the language his audience wanted to hear. Brady recalled that after the speech "several men came up and said, 'Judge, you ought to write that in a book.' I told several men in public office that I was going to wait until June and if nothing was done about the problem, I was going to publish it. Nothing was done, so I put it out."

The book, entitled *Black Monday,* was to be both the acknowledged inspiration for the Citizens' Councils and an uncanny prophecy of future events in Mississippi. A mixture of the author's racial theories with his suggestions on what should or could be done to meet the threat of integration and communism, it is an invaluable introduction to any study of the Citizens' Councils.

In the forward Brady wrote, "Denunciation and abuse are the favorite weapons of the clumsy, frustrated and uncontrolled. I shall strive to proceed without them, but impartial frankness and truth should not be confused with bitter criticisms and reproach." He then clearly established his central thesis in the opening pages of the first chapter. He wrote, "What happened in India and in Egypt happened in Babylon—it happened in Burma, Siam, in Greece, Rome, and in Spain. It is the same deadly story—the Negroid blood like the jungle, steadily and completely swallowing up everything." The corollary to this was given just as succinctly.

Whenever and wherever the white man has drunk the cup of black hemlock, whenever and wherever his blood has been infused with blood of the Negro, the white man, his intellect and his culture have died. This is as true as two plus two equals four. The proof is that Egypt, India, the Mayan civilization, Babylon, Persia, Spain and all the others have never and can never rise again.

Brady then gave the sequence of the Supreme Court decisions leading up to May 17, 1954, and castigated the Court for departing from all legal precedent in the decision handed down on that day. He wrote on page 44:

27

Oh, High Priests of Washington, blow again and stronger upon the dying embers of racial hate, distrust and envy. Pour a little coal oil of political expediency and hope of racial amalgamation upon the flickering blaze which you have created and you will start a conflagration in the South which all of Neptune's mighty ocean can not quench. The decision which you handed down on Black Monday has arrested and retarded the economic and political and, yes, the social, status of the Negro in the South for at least one hundred years.

In his suggestions for what could be done, Judge Brady had several alternatives. He called for the election of Supreme Court judges and the United States Attorney General, suggested the possible formation of a third party, since he felt that there were not actually two distinct parties in existence, considered the possibility of organizing a group tentatively named the National Federation of Sovereign States of America, and said that "the organization which will ultimately accomplish the aims and purposes of the National Federation of Sovereign States will have to be a 'grass roots' organization." He continued:

It will be the test of tests [the decision on what to do about the public schools] and it will be met if all other plans fail, and if the Communists' front organizations, the CIO and the NAACP should succeed in forcing, against the will of the Negroes and the white people of the South, the integration of the races into our public schools. In this event, the public schools will have to be abolished.

Then followed the judge's darker glimpse into the future.

If trouble is to come, we can predict how it will arise. . . . The fulminate which will discharge the blast will be the young Negro schoolboy or veteran—who has no conception of the difference between a mark and a fathom. The supercilious, glib young Negro, who sojourned in Chicago or New York, and who considers the counsel of his elders archaic, will perform an obscene act, or make an obscene remark, or a vile overture or assault upon some white girl. For they will reason . . . "we need but to assert ourselves and abolish every last vestige of segregation and racial difference." This is the reasoning which produces riots, raping and revolutions.

To forestall such an eventuality, the judge offered at least one possibility. He said:

As a last resort, a step which no Southern man wants to take, is declaring of a cold war and an economic boycott. . . . A great many Negro employees will be discharged, and though it will work a grave hardship on many white employers, still it is better "if our right eye offend us to pluck it out." . . . The Negro of the South should be forewarned, and when the next case is brought in in any of the remaining thirteen states, the economic boycott should begin. The irony of the African proverb, "Full belly boy says to empty belly boy, be of good cheer," should be explained to the Southern Negro.

The South did indeed have some black marks against it for its treatment of the Negro in the past and they should be rectified, the judge said, but the basic position of the Negro should still remain inferior to that of the white. The superiority of the white race was nowhere better represented than in its women and children, he said. "The loveliest and purest of God's creatures, the nearest thing to an angelic being that treads this terrestrial ball is a well-bred, cultured Southern white woman or her blue-eyed, golden-haired little girl." It was between the "chimpanzee [by inference, the Negro] who had been taught some tricks" and the "purest of God's creatures" that the battle lines were to be drawn.

One man who read Judge Brady's book was Robert Patterson, a planter in the Mississippi Delta's Sunflower County. The effect it had upon him was galvanic. Before the Supreme Court decision, Patterson's interests had seemingly been only those of an ordinary Delta planter. A native of Clarksdale, Mississippi, he had attended Mississippi State College where he was captain of the football team in 1942. After service in the Army during World War II he had returned to the state and had settled down to farm some land he rented near Indianola.

Earlier than the publication of *Black Monday*, however, Patterson's racial views had been articulated in some strange sources. Before and immediately after the Supreme Court decision, letters and articles appeared under his signature in several distinctly anti-Semitic publications. B'nai B'rith's official magazine, *Facts*, in January 1956 carried an article which said:

Before the Citizens' Councils were officially launched, Pyle's anti-Semitic "Political Reporter" listed Patterson as a "staff writer." Articles under Patterson's by-line appeared in four issues that year (Feb., March, May, and Aug.). A piece by Patterson also appeared in the March–April issue of the "National Renaissance Bulletin," the hate sheet published by the neo-Nazi, James Madole. And Bryant Bowles' "National Forum" (Sept., '54), contained a letter from Patterson.

Nevertheless, Patterson later told Judge Brady that it had been *Black Monday* which had been the catalyst in his decision to devote his life to the battle for racial segregation. The exact time sequence after Patterson read the book is uncertain, but sometime in early July he and five other men got together in Indianola and formed the nucleus of the first Citizens' Council. Included in this group were Arthur Clark, a prominent local attorney now a Circuit Court judge; Herman Moore, a local banker; and Patterson. Indianola is in Sunflower County, the home of Senator James O. Eastland, which may have something to do with the theory advanced in an article in the NAACP magazine, *The Crisis*, that the Councils were really first organized by the senator on June 26, 1954, in Forest, Mississippi. There does not seem to be any basis for this, however, and the later time and place is generally accepted.

From this early July gathering came a larger one on July 11 when fourteen men met in a private residence. The Citizens' Council's first *Annual Report* of August 1955 said of this meeting:

In July, 1954, the first Citizens' Council was formed in Indianola by 14 men, who met and counselled together on the terrible crisis precipitated by the United States Supreme Court in its Black Monday decision of May 17, 1954. For the first time in American history, racial segregation, the way of life regulating the daily activities of tens of millions of American citizens, black and white, in a well known pattern of familiar and satisfactory conduct, has been declared illegal.

The basic organizational framework for the Council worked out at this meeting was to become the standard for all Councils organized thereafter. There were four committees, Membership and Finance, Legal Advisory, Political and Elections, and Information and Education. "Within the scope of these four fields of activity lies the real heart and muscle of the Citizens' Council," the report said.

One of the Council's first recruiting circulars went into thorough detail on what each committee was expected to do. It stated:

1. Political and Elections Committee—Screen all candidates in local and state elections against those who might be seeking the Negro vote. If necessary, organize a white private election within our group to combat the Negro bloc vote (as our old white primary). Discourage Negro registration by every legal means.

2. Information and Education Committee—Gather information pertaining to segregation from all over our nation. Seek facts to present to our people. Educate all

citizens, black and white, to the advantages of segregation and the dangers of integration. Handle press, radio and speakers. Coordinate with other similar organizations.

3. Membership and Finance Committee—Seeks white patriotic voters for membership. We must mobilize public opinion.

4. Legal Advisory Committee—Anticipates moves by agitators and devise legal means for handling any problems that may arise. Provide legal council for all members. Recommend application of economic pressure to troublemakers.

Further details were also worked out, according to the *Annual Report.*

The idea of solid and unified backing of circuit clerks, sheriffs, and local and state officials in the proper discharge of sworn duties was worked out. The concept of assembling non-political community leadership into a unified body to provide the best thinking on the local level, dealing with local problems, became deeply rooted.

It was acknowledged that the impending threat was of such magnitude that our elected officials would be unable to deal with it without the unyielding and organized support of thousands of responsible white citizens to counter the steadily mounting pressure and unceasing attacks from left-wing groups, which were and are liberally financed, skilled in revolutionary techniques that are literally a closed book to most of our political leaders, and irrevocably dedicated to our destruction.

Shortly after this meeting there was another with some 70 persons attending. Here men were selected in pairs to go into other counties to explain the purpose of the Council. In less than six weeks the organization was established in 17 nearby counties. Most of the initial work was done in secrecy, a necessity which co-founder Herman Moore explained at one of the early meetings:

> There has been no publicity and we suggest to each group that they keep it out of the papers and off the air. The news has trickled out, just as we had expected and hoped it would. The Negroes know that we are organizing, but he [sic] does not know what we plan to do. The best thing, we think, is to put him where he has stayed for 40 years and keep him guessing, and continue our efforts.

As the idea spread, the devices used to hasten that expansion were improved upon by the original leaders. One of the standard techniques was the use of form letters which were sent to thousands of white citizens throughout the Delta inviting them to attend quasi-secret meetings in Indianola. The tape recorder was also extensively used. On one tape cut for use at meetings of men interested in the formation of a Citizens' Council in their own communities, Arthur Clark identified the forces to be fought by all "right-thinking" Mississippians. These included the NAACP, politicians and parties catering to the Negro bloc vote, a considerable part of the national (and occasionally local) leadership of the Protestant and Roman Catholic churches, and large segments of the press. He also advocated the use of economic pressure against any dissenters or "troublemakers" in the community.

Perhaps the organizational technique most often employed was to have a Citizens' Council sympathizer in an unorganized community maneuver an invitation for some well-known Citizens' Council figure such as Judge Brady or Jackson attorney John Satterfield to speak to a local civic club. After this talk the local Citizens' Council backer (or backers) would arrange for a meeting of all those who had expressed interest in the speaker's point of view, and again a prominent Citizens' Council member would address them, this time stressing more heavily the need for a Citizens' Council in that community. Short film clips were widely used at these meetings, all emphasizing the job the Citizens' Council had done to stop the Communist plot for integration. Thereafter the existence of a Council in that community was assured.

During the period that the Citizens' Councils were taking their first tentative steps toward expansion, events in Mississippi were working in such a way as to enhance greatly their future growth. On July 30, Governor Hugh White called the state's first modern-day state-level biracial meeting to seek endorsement from the state's Negro leaders of a "voluntary" segregation plan, contingent on the state's immediate commencement of a building program to wipe out the estimated 115 million dollar disparity between white and Negro school facilities. Out of an estimated 90 Negro leaders present, only one endorsed the plan. The others, led by Dr. T. R. M. Howard, of the all-Negro town of Mound Bayou, issued a statement to the press that they were "unalterably opposed to any effort of either white or Negro citizens to attempt to circumvent the decision of the Supreme Court of the United States of America outlawing segregation in public schools."

Governor White was apparently startled by this reply, because in his statement to the press at the conclusion of the meeting he said:

I am stunned. I have believed that the vast majority of Negroes would go along. Now I am definitely of the opinion you can't put faith in any of them on this proposition.

On the same day, after the Negroes had taken their position, he called a conference of the Legal Education Advisory Commission, which voted unanimously to have the governor call a special session of the legislature on September 7, 1954, to consider a constitutional amendment to give the legislature the power to abolish the public school system. Charles Hills, of the Jackson *Clarion-Ledger,* had written off this proposal earlier in June. He said then:

After weeks of great secrecy, that hoodless Ku Klux Klan, the Legal Advisory Committee on Education, comes forth with a brainstorm that actually bowls us over. They tell us that they have decided to abolish the public school system. Are we really in the dangerous place that requires departure from the foundation rock of a public school system?

The LEAC apparently thought so (and, incidentally, newsman Hills was soon to think so too) and so did the white educators of the state after a warning from Governor White that if they did not support the amendment, they wouldn't receive any funds for the school year of 1955–56. He could accomplish this, he said, by refusing to reconvene the legislature to provide the funds which had not been appropriated in its last session. The educators were further promised that if they did support the amendment, the equalization program would be put into effect.

There was little positive Negro activity in this period. A petition was presented to the Walthall County School Board by 30 Negroes asking for immediate integration, but when some whites protested, all 30 withdrew their names immediately. Some of them protested that they had not understood the petition's contents and had thought that it merely asked for equal school facilities.

By late summer 1954, the existence of the Citizens' Councils was an open secret in the Delta. In an editorial on September 6, the Greenville *Delta Democrat-Times* stated:

Reports which we have heard which we believe . . . reliable, [indicate] these groups being formed for the purpose of maintaining the status quo are among the most respectable citizens in each community. If that is true, then the only unresponsible aspect of the organizations is their secrecy. It's time to come out into the open, gentlemen.

The publicity surrounding the mailing of a form letter by Robert Patterson to potential members played a large part in bringing the Councils to closer public scrutiny. In it was a list of selected reading material which he recommended, and he explained why some of the items had been included.

Some of these groups are anti-Semitic; however, all of the religious groups, including all Protestant, Catholic, and Jewish, have been pushing the anti-segregation issue and it is time for all of us to speak out for separation of the black and white races, regardless of our race or creed.

Some of the publications were indeed very anti-Semitic, though most of them were also anti-Negro. Included were *The American Nationalist,* the *Christian Nationalist Crusade, Common Sense, The White Sentinel,* and a number of others. In a later interview Patterson would not discuss the letter, neither denying nor admitting he sent it, but he did state emphatically that "we are not anti-Semitic."

Three days after its editorial calling on the Councils to "come out into the open," the *Delta Democrat-Times* carried a story headed "CC Members Speak out on Organization's Aims." The mayor of the neighboring town of Leland, William Caraway, was quoted as saying that "we are trying a peaceful and intelligent approach to a very difficult problem. Somebody has to be a spokesman for the majority of the white people, and it is a lot better to have that somebody be on the side of reason and the law."

Another member in Leland said:

> We want the people assured that there is responsible leadership organized which will and can handle local segregation problems. If that is recognized, there will be no need for any "hot-headed" bunch to start a Ku Klux Klan. If we fail, though, the temper of the public may produce something like the Klan.

The stated aims of "The Citizens' Committee" of Leland were also given to the paper. These included the maintenance of segregation, the prevention of violence between the races, and the reactivation of states' rights.

The Citizens' Councils were now fully in the open; and on September 13, on the floor of the Mississippi House of Representatives, Representative Wilma Sledge of Indianola explained the existence and purpose of the Councils. She said:

> The Citizens' Councils are a widespread group of local organizations composed of reliable white male citizens who believe that segregation is not discrimination and are organized for the sole purpose of maintaining segregation of the races.

> The existence and purpose of each Council is non-secretive; however, there are some operations of the Councils which for obvious reasons cannot be published. Such operations will be legal.

> It is not the intent or purpose of the Citizen Councils to be (or to be used as) a political machine.

I am sure that you agree with me that such motives and methods are laudable, timely and impressive. They deserve the sanction and participation of all who are willing to mutually pledge their lives, their fortunes, and their honor to the preservation of an unsullied race. To falter would be tragic; to fail would be fatal. They will neither falter nor fail.

The United Press carried a story on the Councils on September 18, giving little more than the fact of their existence and the organization of a typical Council, but it did bring the Councils to public notice outside the borders of the state.

Meanwhile, the legislature, meeting in special session from September 7–30, voted overwhelmingly to present the proposed constitutional amendment for the abolishment of the public school system to the people on December 21, 1954. The proposed amendment gave the legislature the power to abolish the schools by a two thirds vote—but only if it seemed that integration was inevitable either state-wide or locally. During this same session one "segregation" bill was passed which made citizens subject to prosecution for conspiracy if two or more plotted to overthrow or violate the segregation laws of the state through force, violence, threats, intimidations, or otherwise.

The Citizens' Councils immediately pledged full support for the school amendment. An Association of Citizens' Councils of Mississippi, claiming organizations in 20 counties, had been established in Winona on October 12,

1954. Robert Patterson was elected executive secretary. One of the association's first actions was to offer financial assistance to the Legal Education Advisory Committee to publicize the campaign for the amendment. There had been an attempt made in the legislature to have the state furnish the money for this purpose, but the measure had failed by a close vote. The Council's proposal was tendered through Walter Sillers, the speaker of the House of Representatives and a member of the LEAC, but the LEAC rejected the offer, suggesting that those interested in supporting the amendment handle their own campaigns.

The State Executive Committee of the Citizens' Councils decided to do so, but before the campaign for this measure could begin, another amendment came before the people in November. This amendment, one of the measures passed in the regular session of the legislature in early 1954, required that a citizen, in order to qualify to vote, had to be able to read and write, and write in his own hand a "reasonable" interpretation of the state constitution. The state had rejected a similar amendment in 1952, but in November 1954 it passed this one by a vote of 75,488 to 15,718. In its first *Annual Report,* the Association of the Citizens' Councils declared:

> The first major accomplishment and the first project undertaken by our Councils on a state level was the passage of the Constitutional Amendment to raise voter qualification in Mississippi. Although the same amendment failed to pass in 1952, it passed by a tremendous

41

majority when the people of Mississippi, through the Citizens' Councils, were informed of the necessity and reason for the passage of this amendment. It is impossible to estimate the value of this amendment to future peace and domestic tranquility in this state.

The election results can in large part be dismissed as a vote of reaction after the Supreme Court decision, since the voters most affected by the amendment would be the mass of Negroes in the state. Nevertheless, it is true that the largest voter turnout was in those counties where the Citizens' Councils were already organized. In Sunflower County, home of the Councils, not one of the 114 qualified Negro voters went to the polls, despite the fact that the amendment was obviously aimed at curbing their right to vote.

The Councils were now newsworthy enough to make the New York *Times*. On November 21, deep in the first section, a story appeared under the headline, "Integration Foes Arise in the South." It said that "a new type of anti-Negro vigilante movement—using boycotts instead of bull whips—has arisen in at least one state in the South." It quoted Dr. Emmett J. Stringer, a dentist in Columbus, Mississippi, and president of the state NAACP, as saying that one local president of the NAACP had already been forced out. "As for me," he said, "I can't get credit anywhere in Mississippi, and I'm just getting started." The rest of the story was a meager outline of the Councils' history.

During the same month the Citizens' Councils Association published a pamphlet entitled *The Citizens' Council*. The lead paragraph of this five-page publication said:

The Citizens' Council is the modern version of the old-time town meeting called to meet any crisis by expressing the will of the people. The right to peaceably assemble to petition for redress of grievances is guaranteed in the first one of our Bill of Rights in the Constitution of the United States of America. The only reliable prophet for the future is the past, and history proves that the Supreme Power in the government of men has always been Public Sentiment. The Citizens' Council simply provides the machinery for mobilizing, concerting and expressing public opinion.

The pamphlet continued:

The Citizens' Council is the South's answer to the mongrelizers. We will not be integrated! We are proud of our white blood and our white heritage of sixty centuries. . . . If we are bigoted, prejudiced, un-American, etc., so were George Washington, Thomas Jefferson, Abraham Lincoln, and other illustrious forebears who believed in segregation. We choose the old paths of our founding fathers and refuse to appease anyone, even the internationalists.

It concluded with a statement containing the central theme of the pamphlet.

At this time there are one hundred and ten towns in Mississippi that now have Citizens' Councils, including over 25,000 white male members and penetrating 33

43

counties. Our sister states, Alabama and Georgia, have formed councils and they are now spreading. A state Association of Mississippi has been formed with headquarters at Greenwood, Mississippi. (Moved from Winona.) Our councils have helped pass a vital amendment to our state constitution, that the people of Mississippi failed to pass only two years ago. Racial tensions have been eased and local problems solved in counties that have active Citizens' Councils.

With these 25,000 members apparently in full accord, the State Association then moved into battle for the school amendment. Opposing those who joined the Councils in favoring the amendment were a handful of legislators (most of whom were included in the "Friends of Segregated Schools" organization, led by Miss Alma Hickman and Representative Joel Blass of Stone County), two or three newspapers, the NAACP, and an unknown part of the voting public. Large segments of the state's group of educators had been either coerced or won over to support of the measure by the threats and promises of Governor White noted above. Representative Blass, speaking for part of the opposition forces, said that the amendment was "Delta inspired," was backed by those who had always been opponents of the public school system, and would be used to abolish the school system immediately after passage. The charge that the measure was a Delta measure had enough truth to it to make it seem believable, since the heaviest burden of any equalization program would fall on the richer Delta counties rather than the poorer hill sections. Thus, if its proponents in truth intended to use it to abolish the public school system immediately, the Delta would come off best economically. Representative Blass's statement, however, had the immediate effect of highlighting the traditional political split in Mississippi between the plantation Delta, with its high proportion of Negroes, and the "Hills," an all-embracing term for the rest of the state characterized primarily by white farmers of small plots of land.

Despite the heated campaign, on December 21, in a vote marked by widespread apathy (only one third of the qualified voters bothered to cast their ballots) the citizens of Mississippi voted by a 2–1 margin to give the legislature the power to abolish the public school system. According to the *Southern School News* of January 1955, the 26 counties with known Citizens' Councils went overwhelmingly for it, with majorities in only 14 counties—none in the Delta—voting against it. The *Annual Report* of the Councils, in commenting on this, said:

Our next major effort was the school amendment. On December 21 of last year the people of Mississippi passed the amendment that gave the Legislature the power to abolish the public schools as a last resort in order to prevent racial integration in these schools. In passing this amendment we told the world in no uncertain terms that before we would submit to integration we would abolish our schools and set up state-supported private schools. Against organized opposition the Citizens' Councils threw their strength behind the

45

passage of this bill. The Council officers felt that if integration came to Mississippi our schools would automatically be destroyed, and they felt that this amendment was merely a legal statement of principle and fact that expressed the sentiment of the people of Mississippi.

It is somewhat doubtful, however, how decisive the Councils' support was to the passage of the amendment in reality, or how strong the opposition was to it. Election figures show that in eight counties which were not organized by the Citizens' Council as late as 1957, the vote at least matched the state percentage of 2–1 in favor of the bill, and in another unorganized county the amendment also passed, though by a slim majority.

It might be nearer to the truth to say that the percentage of Negroes in each county had more to do with how the county went than any other single factor. Lee and Pearl River counties, the home counties of two of Mississippi's former racist demagogues, are a case in point. The two counties both had a long history of racial ill-feeling, but both had comparatively low Negro percentages in their populations. Lee County, the home ground of former United States Representative John Rankin, had only 27.8 per cent Negroes and went 5–1 against the amendment. Pearl River County, the late Senator Theodore Bilbo's home county, with only 21.7 per cent Negroes, went approximately 2–1 against the amendment. In only one county which went against the amendment was the percentage of Negroes any higher than 30 per cent, that county being Benton County with 43.7 per cent Negroes.

On the other hand, the counties with the highest density of Negro population overwhelmingly approved the amendment. Largely concentrated in the Delta, where the proportion of Negroes to whites sometimes reaches 4–1, as in Tunica County, and is nowhere lower than approximately 3–2, these counties gave lopsided majorities in favor of the amendment as high as 100–1.

No matter what the basic reasons for the passage of the amendment may have been, however, the Council had distinguished itself by its public and unceasing support for it, and deserved at the very least a good part of the credit it took upon itself. This alone was enough to establish the fact that in five short months the Citizens' Council movement had grown to be a highly potent force. Two months later Hodding Carter, editor of the *Delta Democrat-Times* and one of the few whites vocally opposing the Councils in the state, was forced to admit this fact. He wrote:

The third fact is that in the first six months of the Councils' existence they have won each fight they've entered, or objective they've sought, without physical violence. Most of the vocal Negro opposition to continued segregation in Mississippi has been silenced. The two amendments designed to keep the Negro in his traditional place have been one-sidedly approved. Not a single office seeker in a state which will hold statewide elections this summer has publicly criticized the Councils, even though some have privately wrung their hands over their actions. And the offensive by

47

duplicating machines has—as I know—isolated the relatively few white citizens who have spoken out against the Councils.

Thus the end of 1954 found the Citizens' Councils in an excellent position for even greater expansion than they had experienced previously. In the following three years they were to make full use of that position.

CHAPTER III

The Citizens' Councils and Mississippi Politics
(1955-58)

The Citizens' Council is definitely a non-partisan organization and is not engaged in politics. There's no reason to be in politics in Mississippi for the Citizens' Council because there is no disagreement among candidates. Of course, on certain occasions the Citizens' Council has taken a stand, but these were primarily local instances. The Citizens' Council is simply not a political organization.

William Simmons, Editor, *The Citizens' Council*

IN ANNOUNCING the formation of the Citizens' Councils Representative Wilma Sledge had said on the floor of the Mississippi legislature in September 1954 that "it is not the intent or purpose of the Citizens' Councils to be used as a political machine." During the first months of the

Councils' growth this view was echoed by most of its spokesmen. Nevertheless, the Councils had already entered politics, at the very least as strong lobbyists, by the end of 1954 when they took the lion's share of the credit for the passage of the two constitutional amendments already reviewed.

A reporter for the New York *Herald Tribune* probably hit the nail on the head when he wrote, "Though it [the Citizens' Council] makes a big point in insisting that it is not political, it certainly is a political action group. It openly is putting its weight behind all politicians who favor its program." For the next three years the Council was to engage with increasing frequency in such "political action."

During the early months of 1955 the legislature was in session to devise ways to finance the school equalization program. It worked from January to the first of April to produce an acceptable financing scheme and in the process had time for little else. William Simmons, the editor of the Citizens' Council state-wide paper, recently claimed that the "school equalization program was supported by the Councils," but at the time no such claims were made publicly by any member of the Councils and there does not appear to be any proof for this statement. At any rate, a tax measure was agreed upon by the legislature and it adjourned supposedly until its regular session in January 1956.

Political activity in the state was relatively dormant from then until the Supreme Court's implementation decision of May 31, 1955. The reaction of the state to that decision was mixed, a few praising the moderation of the Court, others stating flatly that nothing less than a reversal of the earlier ruling would have been acceptable. Just prior to the ruling Senator Eastland had begun presenting in Congress his thesis that the "Supreme Court has been influenced and infiltrated by Reds," which he continued sporadically through 1958. And immediately after the decision the Legal Education Advisory Committee reaffirmed its opposition to desegregation in any form whatsoever. The rest of Mississippi's congressional delegation, all Democrats in the state's one-party tradition, were no less emphatic in their defense of segregation, Congressman John Bell Williams being the most vocal in his defiance of the Supreme Court.

The segregation controversy provided more grist for the political mill that summer. A hell-for-leather gubernatorial fight was being waged (victory in the Democratic primary being tantamount to election) by five candidates who were, as seems traditional in Mississippi, vying as to who had the best segregationist record. All five appeared together for the first and only time of the campaign to speak to a "non-political" Citizens' Council rally held at Canton, and all five assured the crowd that segregation would be maintained in Mississippi, no matter who won. Mississippi's Attorney General J. P. Coleman, who would be the successful candidate, spoke for them all when he declared that he was "thoroughly ready for anything those who wish to destroy segregation may wish to come up with."

After the day's activities, Robert Patterson remarked to

a reporter that "we have four kings and a queen" (one of the candidates being a woman) to choose from for governor. However, the reporter later noticed when he went through his notes that all of the candidates except Coleman had heaped praise upon the Councils, a fact apparently unnoticed by Patterson, who refused to comment on the story after it appeared.

Despite his studied failure to endorse the Councils, J. P. Coleman, although written off in the early election prognosticating, drew enough votes to enter the runoff with Paul Johnson, the son of a former governor and a perennial candidate for governor himself. Again most of the "smart money" was placed against Coleman. Certainly events in Mississippi at the time seemed to indicate that the candidate who most strongly stated his position as an ardent segregationist would be elected. At this, Paul Johnson was a past master.

Among the elements which contributed to the heat of the campaign, the issue of Negro voting and Negro rights was the most incendiary. The chairman of the state Democratic committee had specifically challenged the right of Negroes to vote in the Democratic primary, since, he said, "Negroes might be national Democrats but were not Mississippi Democrats." He concluded by saying that "We don't intend to have Negroes voting in this primary, but we also intend to handle it in a sensible orderly manner." After this warning, few Negroes attempted to vote. In some of the communities where they did try, they were systematically barred by the local registrars. Robert Patterson, speaking for the Citizens' Councils, had said that he had "no objection" to the Negroes voting, but there were complaints nevertheless that Citizens' Council pressure was keeping the Negroes from voting.

In the meantime, the NAACP had filed a petition for desegregation of the public schools in Vicksburg, which it followed very closely with similar ones in Clarksdale, Natchez, Jackson, and Yazoo City. All of these petitions were filed before the first primary, all brought loud shouts from the gubernatorial candidates of "political motivation," and all undoubtedly accounted for a large part of the sudden swell in Citizens' Council membership, which by mid-August was about 60,000.

Frederick Sullens, writing in the Jackson *Daily News,* declared:

> On Monday, the National Association for the Advancement of Colored People, the radical Negro organization dominated by Communist-front leaders, threw down the gage of battle at Vicksburg. The NAACP states it will file similar petitions demanding the ending of segregation in the public schools in Jackson, Clarksdale and Natchez by August 1.
>
> There is only one way to meet the attack of the NAACP. Organized aggression must be met by organized resistance.
>
> If you believe that segregation provides the only stable arrangement for mutual respect and right conduct between the races, then you owe it to yourself . . . to get

53

in touch immediately with the Jackson Citizens' Council headquarters in the Walthall Hotel and JOIN NOW.

The clock is about to strike. It is already 11:30.

The possibilities of 60,000 Citizens' Councils members swinging in a bloc to the candidate who wooed them best must have been evident to both men in the second primary, but only Paul Johnson publicly sought such bloc support. In one speech he linked Coleman to retiring Governor Hugh White, whom he characterized as "ineffectual in the racial crisis," and said that the Councils were made of "fine Mississippians who had banded together into the Citizens' Councils to maintain segregation because they felt the governor and state leadership were too weak to deal with the situation." He implied that Coleman would also be "weak" and that only he could fill the expectations of the Citizens' Councils' rank and file.

Whether Johnson's quest for the Citizens' Council vote was heeded by the average member or not, no candidate was publicly endorsed by the State Executive Committee of the Councils, and Johnson lost to Coleman in a record turnout of voters on August 23. Coleman immediately made a "solemn pledge" that "there will be no necessity to abolish the public schools, nor will there be any mixing of the races in these schools.

Shortly after the election the LEAC adopted a Coleman-sponsored six-point program for consideration by the legislature (Coleman, *like* Speaker Sillers, was a member of the Advisory Committee). These included bills to make "stirring up litigation" a violation of state law, to repeal the state's compulsory school attendance law, and to create a permanent "authority for the maintenance of racial segregation" with a full staff and funds for its operation to come out of tax money. The Jackson Citizens' Council promptly passed a resolution endorsing all of the program and calling upon the legislature for its immediate passage.

At this time (September 1955) an idea which several Citizens' Council leaders had been considering came to fruition. Robert Patterson first brought it to public notice when he wrote in the *Annual Report*:

> For quite some time your Directors have been studying the feasibility of a newspaper for the Citizens' Councils. They have long realized that a paper would be the very best medium possible for the dissemination of news for and about your Council.
>
> This newspaper would have still been in the "studying stage" had it not been that Mr. W. J. "Bill" Simmons, unpaid Administrator of the State Council and secretary of the Jackson Citizens' Council, offered at a meeting of the board of directors on Tuesday, August 25, 1955, to edit this paper without salary. Your directors fell all over themselves to accept this proposition.

The first issue of the paper, named *The Citizens' Council*, was published in October 1955. A four-page monthly tabloid, it is devoted to whatever current race or segregation-integration issue seems important to Simmons or the State Executive Committee. The first issue was self-laudatory, carrying long articles borrowed from previous works by such men as Tom Waring, editor of the Charleston *News and Courier,* and John Temple Graves, a syndicated Southern columnist. All were loud in praise of the Councils and equally loud in denunciation of their enemies. In the lead article it was explained that *The Citizens' Council* would be offered to all CC members in Mississippi and throughout the nation and to anybody else who might wish to subscribe. The paper carried no advertising, and was to be supported by the two-dollar subscription rate which Simmons recommended be taken out of each member's yearly five-dollar dues.

The first proposal the paper backed was the plan for interposition proposed at the close of 1955 by Senator Eastland, Congressman Williams, and Judge Brady. The three men jointly recommended that Mississippi follow in the footsteps of several of her sister Southern states and pass a resolution of interposition. Their statement said:

> The time has come in the life of our country for the sovereign States of this Nation to take stock and review their relationship to the Federal Government. Should not the gradual usurpation of the sovereign rights of the States by the Federal Government through illegal decisions by the United States Supreme Court cause the states of this Union to view with concern this trend?
>
> . . . We think the Southern States should carefully consider the doctrine and precedents that a State has the

56

legal right of interposition to nullify, void and hold for naught the deliberate, dangerous and palpable infractions of the Constitution committed by the Supreme Court; infractions that are so great that our system of government is threatened.

The statement then listed all the instances when nullification or interposition had been successfully tried in the United States and suggested that it could be done again. The proposal had the endorsement of the State Executive Committee of the Citizens' Councils, as represented in Tom Brady; *The Citizens' Council;* and the Jackson chapter of the CC (the largest in the state). The Jacksonians presented a resolution to the three co-signers of the proposal which was fairly indicative of the state-wide Citizens' Council feeling on interposition. It said:

The Board of Directors of the Jackson Citizens' Council wish to express to you their strong commendation and endorsement for the recommendations, submitted this day by you gentlemen, that those states of our Union whose laws provide for separation of the races in various aspects of public life give solemn and careful consideration to . . . [an] action of interposition to counteract unlawful usurpation of power by the United States Supreme Court.

In these days of sore travail for our own state and for her co-states, we are blessed to have men of wisdom and courage to chart a course of action in the finest constitutional traditions of our country.

The idea of interposition appealed to many in the state who were willing to use much blunter language than that in the proposal. Representative Williams spoke for these when he declared in the House of Representatives of the United States Congress on January 25, 1956:

Mr. Speaker, I have heard many say that they favor interposition, but are opposed to nullification. This is the same thing as saying that we favor the aiming and firing of our guns but that we are against the hitting of the target.

The very purpose of interposition is to nullify. If that is not to be the purpose, the act of interposition becomes merely an expression of disfavor and is meaningless.

Despite this attitude of some Mississippians and the backing of the Citizens' Council, Governor-elect Coleman, in a talk to the Legal Education Advisory Committee on December 14, 1955, referred to the idea of nullification or interposition as "legal poppycock." He said:

All efforts at nullification have been abject failures . . . all it would do would invite the President to send federal troops into Mississippi—and some of them would be Negroes—and certainly Mississippi can't whip the whole United States. The legislature can't close the United States Courts or stop federal processes that way.

Nevertheless, when Coleman took office in January and the legislature had reconvened, his opposition to the principle of interposition had wavered enough for him to sign a declaration of interposition into law with no sign of disagreement. The interposition measure, passed by the legislature in March 1956, said:

[Mississippi] . . . has at no time, through the 14th Amendment to the constitution of the United States, or in any manner whatsoever delegated to the Federal government its right to educate and nurture its youth and its power and right of control over its schools, colleges, education and other public institutions and facilities, and to prescribe the rules, regulations and conditions under which they will be conducted. . . .

It is not within the province of the court to decide the question, because the court itself seeks to usurp the powers which have been reserved to the States, and therefore under these circumstances, the judgment of all the parties to the compact must be sought to resolve the question; that the Supreme Court is not a party to this compact, but a creature of the compact, and the question of contested power cannot be settled by the creature seeking to usurp the power. . . .

The *Second Annual Report* of the Citizens' Councils of Mississippi said of this resolution and other similar ones throughout the South:

The State Legislatures of six Southern States have already passed resolutions of interposition designed to stand between the people of their States and the tyranny of the United States Supreme Court. The Citizens' Council movement in the various states was instrumental in getting these acts passed.

There had been an increasing number of direct attacks upon the Supreme Court and its decisions by various Southern politicians during the period that interposition was becoming a byword in the South. One of the most outspoken of its critics was Senator Eastland. In a typical speech in Senatobia, Mississippi, in August, 1955, he said:

> On May 17, the Constitution of the United States was destroyed because the Supreme Court disregarded the law and decided integration was right. . . . You are not required to obey any court which passes out such a ruling. In fact, you are obligated to defy it.

On December 1, the senator followed this up with another speech, this time before the state-wide convention of the Citizens' Councils in Jackson. In addressing this meeting, which included 2000 CC members, 40 state legislators, Congressman Williams, and Governor White, and which notably did not include Governor-elect Coleman, Eastland said:

> The Supreme Court of the United States, in the false name of law and justice, has perpetrated a monstrous crime. It presents a clear threat and present danger, not only to the law, traditions, customs, and racial integrity of Southern people, but also to the foundation of our Republican form of Government.

> The anti-segregation decisions are dishonest decisions. Although rendered by Judges whose sworn duty it is to

uphold the law and to protect and preserve the Constitution of the United States, these decisions were dictated by political pressure groups bent upon the destruction of the American system of government, and the mongrelization of the white race.

He went on to recommend a Southern regional commission, financed by tax money, to publicize the fight against those "political pressure groups," which run, he said, "from the blood red of the Communist Party to the almost equally red of the National Council of Churches of Christ in the U.S.A." *The Citizens' Council* reported at great length upon this speech and suggested the Citizens' Councils should get behind some such regional commission. Indeed, this concept of a regional propaganda center was one which the Citizens' Council was to return to again and again in the next three years.

Part of Eastland's idea was adopted later in the same month when, at a meeting in Memphis on December 28 and 29, a group which took the name of the Federation for Constitutional Government was formed by delegates from 12 Southern states. Included in the state delegations were Senator Eastland, Senator Strom Thurmond of South Carolina, Governor Marvin Griffin of Georgia, six United States Representatives including John Bell Williams, States' Rights leader Leander Perez of Louisiana, and nine former Southern governors. More important for the Citizens' Council, however, was the inclusion on the "Advisory Board" of the Federation of such members of the Mississippi Citizens' Councils Executive Committee as

61

Tom Brady, Fred Jones, Wilburn Hooker, Ellett Lawrence, and W. J. Simmons, along with fellow Citizens' Council member L. O. Crosby and Walter Sillers. The Federation, which had been conceived in a meeting held in Jackson the previous January, elected John U. Barr of New Orleans chairman of the Executive Committee. Barr, a prominent States' Righter in Louisiana in 1948, stated that the purpose of the group was the "preservation of constitutional government." The segregation decisions were "only one of the small facets being used to destroy the Constitution," he said. It was the intended purpose of the Federation to co-ordinate the activities of all the resistance movements across the South, he said, not trying to control them, but merely to influence and help in their work. Senator Eastland's keynote address at the meeting enlarged on Barr's ideas. He said:

> We are about to embark on a great crusade, a crusade to restore Americanism, and return the control of our Government to our people. In addition our organization will carry on its banner the slogan of free enterprise, and we will fight the organizations who attempt with much success to socialize industry and the great medical profession of this country.

The Mississippi legislature followed the formation of this group with its own answer to Senator Eastland's call for an organization to combat the "Red pressure groups." As the implementing agency of the resolution of interposition, a State Sovereignty Commission was established in early 1956 to "do and perform any and all acts and things deemed necessary and proper to protect the sovereignty of the state of Mississippi and her sister states from encroachment thereon by the Federal government or any branch, department, or agency thereof."

Governor Coleman was named chairman of the commission, which included Attorney-General Joe Patterson, Lieutenant Governor Carroll Gartin, Senators Earl Evans and William Burgin, Representatives Walter Sillers, Joe Hopkins, George Payne, and W. H. Johnson, and three lawyers, Hugh B. Clayton, George Thornton and W. S. Henley. Coleman, in an introductory talk to the commission, said, "After all, integration came about because the people gave up. We will not give up."

The Sovereignty Commission was in great part the product of the governor's thoughts on what the state needed in the way of an anti-integration agency. It was voted $250,000 by the legislature for its work, and an investigation division, specifically Coleman's idea, was set up as an integral part of the commission. This division, under Leonard Hicks, former chief of the state highway patrol, was empowered to employ secret investigators and paid informers. In recommending this division, Coleman had said it was necessary so "we can be ready for all counter-attacks." Speaker of the House Walter Sillers, in a speech in McComb, Mississippi, in April, said that the commission was going to co-operate with the Citizens' Councils, which he described as "the greatest forces we have in this battle to save the white race from amalgamation, mongrelization and destruction."

Governor Coleman, despite his sponsorship of the commission, apparently had a different concept of its operation once it was established from that of Walter Sillers'. When the legislature voted for the commission many legislators envisioned it as serving as a counter agency to the NAACP; but when the NAACP did not follow through on any of its school integration suits of 1955, this aspect of its purpose vanished. The secret agents were probably not used (there being no record as of January 1959 that they were), and the primary function of the commission became that of a study and propaganda center.

In fact, the chief contribution of the Sovereignty Commission in its first three years of existence came through the efforts of its public relations director, Hal Decell, a former Delta newspaperman who had been an early enemy of the Citizens' Councils. Through his salesmanship, a group of New England editors were persuaded to tour Mississippi from October 6, 1956, to October 14, the purpose, according to Decell, being "to breach the wall of sensational journalism which has stood for so long between the South and a national understanding of its problems." In this the project was successful, for though not many of the editors came away convinced of the righteousness of Mississippi's racial position, most did evidence a far better understanding of its roots in the editorials and stories they wrote upon their return home.

However, such projects which were basically oriented around the Coleman administration's policy of "friendly persuasion" did not prove to be exactly what Walter Sillers or the Citizens' Councils had in mind for the Sovereignty Commission, a fact which was to become evident within a year.

One measure which failed to pass, among those considered by the 1956 session of the legislature, deserves a glance as an indication of the mood of the lawmakers. This was House Bill 34, which would have extended "the laws of libel, defamation, and slander so as to prevent libeling, slandering, and defaming states, counties, cities, communities, their inhabitants, their institutions, and their government." Defamatory matter was defined as "any work or statement, oral or written, not libel or slander, but which nevertheless, if true, would tend to expose a person to hatred, etc. . . ." Governor Coleman said he saw nothing wrong with the bill, which had been sponsored by Walter Sillers and six other representatives, but it died in the Senate after being recommitted.

The legislature adjourned, having shored up the state's defenses against any immediate integration, its course of action being made smoother by a temporary compromise of differences between Speaker Sillers and Governor Coleman. The legislature had been joined in its resistance to the Supreme Court desegregation decision by 96 United States congressmen, including the entire Mississippi delegation, on March 12, 1956, who declared in a "Manifesto" that the integration decrees were unconstitutional and announced that they intended to have them reversed by whatever legal means available. The result of the ruling, the congressmen said, had been to destroy amicable relations between the white and Negro races and to replace friendship and understanding with "hatred and suspicion."

The April issue of *The Citizens' Council* carried highly favorable articles on the Manifesto and quoted at length from an article in the Charleston *News and Courier*. It said, "Obviously political pressure was behind the Court's ruling. Political strength is in the hands of the 96 Southern Congressmen if they care to use it."

The Citizens' Councils' *Second Annual Report* in August 1956 asserted that the Citizens' Council had been partly responsible for the Manifesto. It said:

> March 12, 1956, was a historic occasion. This was the day that 101 Southern Congressmen and Senators signed the now famous "Declaration of Constitutional Principles," which made such an impact upon this Nation. The presentation of this document occurred twenty-two months after the Supreme Court's decision. It took that long for public sentiment to be felt in the halls of the Congress of these United States. The Citizens' Council is proud of the part it played in the expression of this sentiment against the tyrannical actions of the Supreme Court.

The Citizens' Councils were soon engaged in a much more important campaign, locally, than the "support" they had given to the Manifesto. The campaign's indirect target was Governor Coleman, though it was not aimed directly at him, and its intent was to establish a third party in Mississippi once more.

The background for this expression of animosity was not hard to find. Ever since the second primary the governor had been making statements designed to soft-pedal the race issue and to calm the people's fears about immediate integration, a policy at direct variance with that of the Citizens' Councils. In a series of public statements he made it clear that he could not join those who were attempting to keep the people in a constant turmoil about the Supreme Court decision. His inaugural address repeated this. He said:

> The sentiment of Mississippi is unanimous—so we have nothing to fear unless it be "fear itself." I have not the slightest fear that four years hence when my successor assumes his official oath that the separation of the races in Mississippi will be left intact. . . . Let us, then, exercise all possible soundness of judgment, sincerity of purpose, and calmness of mind to the end that we shall not fail.

Later, on March 24, 1956, he seemed to come close to criticizing the Manifesto, the Citizens' Councils, and a large segment of the South's leadership. Comparing the present situation with that of pre-Civil War days, he said:

> Those in positions of responsibility must think things through before they take positions of no return. . . . The greatest need of the time is for cool, clear thinking on racial problems. This is no time to let hotheads make us lose our perspective and go beyond the point of no return.

In May 1956 he told reporters in Jackson that he had not joined the Council because he wanted to be in a position to speak for "all the people." The Citizens' Council soon thereafter launched itself into full opposition to Governor Coleman's stated intentions for the forthcoming state Democratic convention. Late in May the State Executive Committee of the Citizens' Councils sent a resolution to all county Democratic organizations for consideration at their pre-convention caucuses. The resolution would have bound the state's delegation to the national convention to vote only for candidates in full accord with the resolution of interposition of Mississippi; stipulated that those men chosen as delegates would have to support the principles of interposition themselves; and asked that the state convention reconvene after the national convention to assess the results of the convention in the light of Mississippi's institutions and principles. Governor Coleman, who strongly believed in an unbound delegation, said that he would have supported the resolution as long as it merely stated Mississippi's principles, but since it would tie strings to the freedom of the delegation he must oppose it.

There followed a month of county courthouse fighting, with the governor coming out clearly on top. The county Democratic organizations voted overwhelmingly to support Coleman's position, less than 10 adopting the resolution sponsored by the Citizens' Councils. Perhaps the criticism of W. J. Tubb, chairman of the Democratic State Executive Committee, influenced the county organizations.

The Citizens' Councils, he said, were "endangering the fight for segregation" by entering politics and circulating the resolution. On July 16, at the state convention, Governor Coleman won control of the delegation after a last-ditch fight by the supporters of the Citizens' Councils' position. They attempted to force one final battle on the issue of setting August 29 as a time for a post-Chicago state convention. Coleman circumvented a head-on collision on this by promising to call an after-Chicago meeting if one fifth of the 280 state convention delegates so desired, or on the call of a majority of the 18-member State Executive Committee.

As it turned out, no call was issued by anyone after the national convention, and all of Mississippi's congressmen, with the exception of John Bell Williams, who followed his own aspirations on a States' Rights ticket elsewhere, came to the support of the national Democratic ticket. Some of those still disgruntled by the Democratic platform of the candidates did form a group which offered a slate of un-committed electors to the people in November, but they were not strong enough to keep the state from going solidly Democratic. The Citizens' Councils did not officially support this ticket or any other, however, nor was there any mention of its existence in *The Citizens' Council* at any time before the election. An editorial in the September issue did state that the South had not won any of its demands at either convention, but then departed from that subject to stress the necessity of further organization before any success could be expected.

Certainly further organization was one of the high lights of 1956 for the Council. By the middle of the year it could claim 80,000 members in the state and was expanding its activities outside of Mississippi.

The *Second Annual Report* outlined some of these activities.

Members and officials of the State Association have travelled to eleven Southern States telling them what we have accomplished in Mississippi and helping them to organize. We are exchanging ideas and methods to be used in the battle that lies ahead. Citizens' Councils have been formed in Louisiana, Texas, Alabama, Arkansas, Florida, Georgia, South Carolina, Tennessee, and Virginia. Fifteen other states have similar organizations. From everywhere comes encouragement and moral support of our righteous cause.

This field work of the Mississippi Councils' members came to fruition in early 1956, when the state Citizens' Councils helped found a national organization of similar organizations.

The first steps toward such a formation were taken on April 7, 1956, when delegates from 11 Southern states, assertedly representing 300,000 Citizens' Councils members, met in New Orleans to form the Citizens' Councils of America. The delegates represented Councils or similar organizations in the states of Alabama, Arkansas, Florida, Georgia, Louisiana, Mississippi, North Carolina, South Carolina, Texas, Tennessee, and Virginia. The Oklahoma

Citizens' Councils had been unable to send a delegation but gave its proxy to Texas. State Senator Rainach of Louisiana was elected chairman of the meeting and presided during the remainder of the convention's proceedings. In a concluding resolution the convention members stated their platform for the future. The resolution said:

> Resolved that we form an organization to be named Citizens' Councils of America for the preservation of the reserved natural rights of the people of the states, including primarily the separation of the races in our schools and all institutions involving personal and social relations; and for the maintenance of our States' Rights to regulate public health, morals, marriage, education, peace and good order in the States, under the Constitution of the United States.

A second convention was held on October 12, 1956, in Jackson, Mississippi. State Senator Sam Englehardt of Alabama presided at this session. The delegates decided that the organization was to function as a co-ordinating and planning agency for the several state associations, and that the Mississippi Council's paper, *The Citizens' Council*, should be adopted as the official paper for all the Councils. Temporary headquarters for the new organization were to be in Greenwood, Mississippi, and Robert Patterson was named executive secretary. Thereafter, the association was to meet semi-annually, its executive board being composed of three members from each state's executive board.

The strategy approved at the convention provided that (1) a sharp counter-attack should be made against the NAACP, (2) the Councils should encourage the people to organize and protest and preserve the separate schools, their social institutions, and their personal rights and liberties, (3) the local Councils should assert the invocation of interposition by the states to guard and recover their sovereign rights from unconstitutional federal invasions, (4) they should present forcefully and accurately at the national level through all modern methods the cause of constitutional government and freedom of personal association.

In an editorial in the November 1956 issue of *The Citizens' Council*, William Simmons outlined the purpose and scope of the new organization and added:

> The Citizens' Councils of America is restricted from attempting to direct or control any Council or other organization, or any member thereof as to any proposed course of action. . . . As we see it, this is simply a statement of reality as it exists with respect to any group of private citizens, be it large or small, since they possess no legislative or police powers, but solely the powers of persuasion and example.

Nevertheless, Council leaders more and more often talked in other terms, with less emphasis on the lack of control and more emphasis on the strength such an organization could have. In the *Second Annual Report*, Patterson had written, "Forty million white Southerners, or a fraction thereof, if properly organized, can be a power in the Nation, but they must be thoroughly organized from the town and county level up." Simmons himself had visions of something more than the "town meeting" concept when he said:

I think [the Citizens' Council] is much more than a white supremacist group and I think it is much more than a protectionist group. I think it is fundamentally the first real stirrings of a conservative revolt in this country, judging by the responses we've gotten from other states. . . .

In another interview he reiterated this:

Frankly I consider the great swell of membership of the councils to come as much from those sick of the New Deal, Fair Deal, and all the other types of Deals which have sapped our individuality as anything else except the racial thing. . . . The movement is a phenomenal thing, a half million [sic] membership in two years organized all over the South, all representing a fundamental conservative revolt and all organized for action.

This was a step removed from the original publicly expressed opinions of Council leaders in previous years, but it was not the only new road the Councils were taking. In December 1956 the Citizens' Council of Mississippi applied for and received a state charter for a tax-free, non-profit education fund. Simmons said the fund was to "provide propaganda to compete with the opposition," and Ellett Lawrence, the state treasurer of the Citizens'

73

Council, stated that the fund would be similar to the NAACP's tax-exempt education fund. In effect it was to perform the function which the Council's leaders had originally hoped the State Sovereignty Commission would co-operate with them in fulfilling.

A certified public accountant in Greenwood advised the Council that contributions made to the fund would be tax deductible, and a drive for contributions was officially opened in the second half of December. Ellett Lawrence was appointed treasurer, and W. C. Trotter, former financial secretary of the University of Mississippi, was made president of the fund. Lawrence keynoted the drive when he said that "only through the accumulation of large financial resources will Mississippi and other Southern States be in position to compete with the millions of dollars of left-wing money being spent on the drive to integrate the white and colored people."

However, the fund drive was not an immediate success. Two years later, in June 1958, the Citizens' Council carried a plea for money for the fund, and in July 1958 Lawrence had to report in the Council's *Fourth Annual Report* that "so far the exemption has not come through, but we have had no kick-backs on former deductions." He continued:

> We wanted a fund so those people who can contribute in large amounts could get tax exemptions, as this means a great deal to many people.

> We are very careful how we handle the money in the Educational Fund, and there is simply no way for

74

the government to declare it other than tax exempt. We hoped this fund would be attractive to larger contributors. So far we have had only two individuals who have contributed $1000 or more.

We hope to have others.

Actually the only announced use for the money was the provision of scholarships for winners of high school essay contests, an undertaking which will be discussed in a later chapter. Otherwise, all of the financing of Council projects came either from its members' dues or from special fund raising, and its interest in establishing a widespread propaganda machine was diverted into channels which are later noted.

In respect to politics in Mississippi, the closing months of 1956 found the state in a fairly calm frame of mind. The schools were still segregated and unthreatened by any school integration suits. The new Congress and the old President did not seem to present any immediate threat to this status quo, and Governor Coleman continued to soft-pedal the race issue. Other than its efforts on behalf of the new education fund little was heard from the Citizens' Council.

The turn of the new year and the first few months of 1957 saw a similar calm pervading the state. Governor Coleman reiterated the theme, angrily disputed by some Negroes, that there was no repression of Negroes in Mississippi, and that the attention of all Mississippians should be paid to the future rather than the past. Following up this theme, he began to drop ever broader hints

75

that a satisfactory future could be grasped for the state only if its constitution were given a thorough overhaul. These remarks were given a good deal of publicity, but the governor did not seem disposed to follow through on them at the time.

In May the State Sovereignty Commission came back into the news briefly in connection with a problem it had been sitting on for several months. This was the question of whether the state should proceed with plans, formulated by the 1954 legislature, to give the federal government land for the erection of an integrated Veterans Administration Hospital in Jackson. The matter was brought out into the open by the agitation of *The Citizens' Council,* which protested editorially against such an action. The State Executive Committee of the Councils then adopted a resolution stating that Veterans Administration hospital integration was harmful "psychologically" to the "physically helpless war veterans" being treated in it. The executive board petitioned Congress "to cause veterans' hospitals to be operated in conformity with the customs, traditions, and laws of the states wherein they are operated."

The Sovereignty Commission then held a meeting and by a vote of seven to one (the one dissenter being State Senator Earl Evans, an arch-political foe of Coleman and a Council supporter) recommended that the State Building Commission go ahead with plans to give the federal government land for a new Veterans Administration hospital to operate on a non-segregated basis. Coleman, as chairman of the commission, was not able to vote but

76

suggested that he be put on record as favoring the motion. Evans protested that the commission was "created for the purpose of maintaining segregation and now we are becoming a party to creating integration."

In fact, he continued, "Here a state agency created to keep segregation is in the position of being a part in the creation of an integrated facility. We're in the position of either endorsing an integrated facility or denying medical facilities to the veterans of Mississippi."

The governor replied: "That's exactly the position we're in. It would put us in a bad light over the country to deny the veterans these facilities just to prove we're segregationist. . . . There's a great deal of difference between putting grown people together in a hospital and putting children together in a school."

By its vote the Commission cleared the way for the erection of the new integrated hospital, and it became a dead issue as far as the state administration was concerned. However, as late as January 1958, *The Citizens' Council* was still suggesting editorially that a bill should be introduced into Congress to outlaw integrated federal facilities where the mores of the state opposed them. When such a bill did finally appear in the House of Representatives it was quietly referred to committee and left to die.

Through the remaining months of spring and summer, Governor Coleman maneuvered steadily to find support for his rapidly crystallizing plans to call a special session of the legislature to approve a constitutional convention. Early in August, Coleman sent out a "personal memorandum" to the Mississippi legislators. In it he asked for their "non-partisan consideration" of his plan and continued:

I am giving strong consideration to the idea of convening a special session of the legislature about November 1. If the legislature wishes, it could then call a constitutional convention for September 1, 1958. The same act could provide for a legislative constitutional revisory committee composed of an appropriate number of members of each house. . . .

I have no political ambitions in mind. I had rather see our constitution revised for the welfare of our state and to have some small part in bringing it about than to hold any office of any kind, now or hereafter.

The last remark was in answer to the published hints that he would use his success in obtaining a new constitution to launch a campaign to oust Senator Eastland from the Senate in the 1960 senatorial election. He said that he had been convinced of the necessity for a new constitution by his trips to Chicago and New York in search of new industry for Mississippi. "So many of the industrialists mentioned the matter that I was overwhelmingly convinced of the necessity of it, simply from an industrial point of view alone," he added. Moreover, such a change would "absolutely guarantee the separation of the races in the public schools as completely as it is possible to guarantee anything."

With the approaching passage of a Civil Rights Bill in Congress, Coleman in late August started pitching his campaign for a new constitution more and more on a racial basis. He announced plans to call a committee of 82 lawyers, one from each county, to sit down and analyze the rights bill when it passed and then work out plans to circumvent it, which could be included in a new constitution. The Civil Rights Bill was "far more serious than a lot of people realize," he said, "particularly in the very counties where the representatives are now fighting hardest against a constitutional convention." To many it seemed that Coleman was aiming this approach straight at the areas of the Citizens' Councils' greatest strength (and particularly the Delta, the home of Speaker Walter Sillers and Senator James Eastland). This belief was strengthened when Coleman, for the first time since the Canton rally, addressed a Citizens' Council meeting— although it was an Alabama Council. Even so, Coleman at no time mentioned the Council nor the NAACP by name in the course of the talk; but he did say, "We must stop running from every spook from behind every stump. We must banish fear to progress and we must resist the temptation to match wrong with wrong."

Later, the governor suggested to the Calhoun City Rotary Club that with a new constitution the manner in which registration took place in Mississippi could be changed so that a three-man board could take over the functions of the registrar of voters and effectively thwart large-scale Negro voting.

Nevertheless, a formidable amount of opposition was already building up to Coleman's suggestions by the first week in September, particularly among the "Old Guard" faction headed by Walter Sillers and representing the Citizens' Councils on most matters. This group was drawn primarily from the Delta and had been long accustomed to ruling the state with an iron hand as governors came and went (no governor being eligible to succeed himself in Mississippi), and the election of Hill-man Coleman over their opposition had been a shock in itself. Despite the successful working agreement that Sillers and Coleman had maintained during the regular session in 1956, such a far-reaching proposal seemed to threaten their position of state leadership and control even further. The issue was further complicated by the fears of this faction that a new constitution would bring legislative reapportionment and the destruction of their power.

At this point, however, outside forces took a hand and the debate on the necessity for a new constitution was temporarily put aside. Governor Faubus of Arkansas called out the state National Guard to "maintain order" around Little Rock's Central High School, and for the next three weeks the attention of most Mississippians was riveted on that city. The first editorial reactions across the state, when there were any, praised Faubus' actions. However, in an editorial carried on September 9, the *Delta Democrat-Times*, under an editorial entitled "Going Too Far," declared that: "Regardless of how one may personally feel about the desirability of integrated schools, state authority cannot in the long run supersede Federal authority. . . . In discounting the mayor on the local situation, Faubus is himself flouting the very principle on which he says he stands—that local officials are

better acquainted with how to preserve domestic tranquility than higher authority."

Otherwise, the state's newspapers kept up a steady
barrage of praise for Faubus and damnation of the federal
government. The Jackson *Daily News's* editor, Frederick
Sullens, commented, "Governor Faubus is strictly within
his legal rights to use National Guardsmen to prevent
trouble in the public schools of Little Rock. What is now
happening in Arkansas will eventually happen in Mississippi when the NAACP screws up enough courage to
make an attempt to force Negro pupils into white schools."

A few days later Sullens added, "If President Eisenhower and Attorney General Brownell intend to declare
war on Arkansas, we may as well be mobilizing our forces
here in Mississippi. First step in mobilization just now
should be applying for membership in the Citizens'
Council and pledging your financial support." Certainly
the entire Council leadership in Mississippi lined up in
behalf of Governor Faubus; but Governor Coleman had
no comment. A campaign speech he had made in 1955
might have explained why he did not speak out now. He
said then, in commenting on another candidate's plan to
use the "police power" of the state to resist integration,
that it was "so much foolishness." He had added, "[the
Supreme Court has held] that police powers must yield
to its decisions. Reliance upon [that plan] could result
in closing of our schools. . . . Police power is worthless.
The U. S. Supreme Court has said time and time again
that state law must bow to federal law."

As the crisis mounted in Little Rock, however, more

and more voices were heard around the state in support of Governor Faubus. In Forest, Mississippi, a high school official announced that "Dixie" would replace the "Star-Spangled Banner" as a prelude to all home football games because of the Little Rock school controversy. The superintendent said, "At least the crowd can stand in sincere reverence and not in resentment to a reminder of the dictatorial power of federal courts." Later he changed his mind.

The Jackson *State-Times* commented: "From events in the Arkansas capital, only one conclusion seems fundamental: the Governor has established firmly the right and responsibility of a state's chief executive to take whatever action necessary to prevent violence." The Jackson *Clarion-Ledger* said, "His action has not been generally recognized as such, but Governor Orval Faubus followed the broad principle of interposition in calling out National Guard members to cope with the situation at Little Rock."

The entry of federal troops into Little Rock to enforce integration heightened the reaction throughout Mississippi. Shock and anger now characterized the public mood, and it did not take long to express itself. In this the Citizens' Council took a leading part. Immediately after President Eisenhower's appearance on television to explain his action, Jackson TV station WLBT and its affiliated radio station WJDX cut out the national anthem that followed over the national network and interjected a spot advertisement from the Mississippi Citizens' Council which said: "Don't let this happen in Mississippi. Join the Citizens' Council today." The announcer then gave details on how to join. The day after the troops were sent into Little Rock, Senator Eastland addressed a Citizens' Council rally in Belzoni at which the Council officers wore black arm bands "mourning the death of states' rights." Senator Eastland told the group that President Eisenhower had violated the Constitution in sending troops into a state without a request from that state.

Governor Coleman finally broke his silence to issue a public statement which touched lightly on Arkansas and then moved on to Mississippi. In part he said:

> I hope all Mississippians of all races will continue to take just pride in our previous ability to work together for the best interest of all, instead of having our state torn asunder in a manner that cannot benefit anyone. What one obtains by force of the U. S. Army, they have to have the Army to maintain, and troops cannot operate a public school system. . . .

> I repeat what I have so many times previously requested: I ask all the people of Mississippi to keep cool heads and calm minds and leave the solution of these problems to our duly chosen officials, which is the only way it can possibly be done. . . .

> We did not make the mess in Little Rock. Let us not lose our heads and permit it to cause a mess here in Mississippi.

The Citizens' Council membership did not rise significantly during September. Most Mississippians who would

83

join such an organization without the direct threat of integration as a spur apparently had already done so. But Little Rock gave the Council an issue which it continued to exploit through 1957 and 1959. All Citizens' Council mail thereafter carried a stamp with the motto, "Remember Little Rock," which depicted a soldier holding a bayonet at the back of two white girls. Over the course of the next year *The Citizens' Council* carried numerous plugs for "Remember Little Rock" rubber stamps, at two dollars apiece, and auto tags featuring a naked bayonet, which could be obtained through its office or from private dealers in Mississippi.

From that point on, the Citizens' Council was to intensify its attack on "moderation" also, the suspicion and fear of most white Mississippians toward any who did not join wholeheartedly in supporting Governor Faubus providing a fertile ground for such work. It was at members and potential members possessing something less than Governor Coleman's hoped-for "cool heads and cool minds" that the Council aimed most of its material thereafter.

An important point, however, is that with rare exception the Little Rock situation produced a unity of feeling among the whites of Mississippi which the Citizens' Council could and did exploit, but for which it could not claim the credit. The televised spectacle of federal troops enforcing integration at the point of a bayonet was enough to produce such a unity in most Mississippians. The specter of Reconstruction is easily raised.

This unity lasted no longer than the month of September. Governor Coleman called a special session of the legislature the first week in November to consider his plans for a constitutional convention, but before the legislature convened both sides managed to get in some additional licks. Taking cognizance of the Little Rock school problem, Governor Coleman told one audience that "if Mississippi doesn't wipe clean its educational slate as presently written in the Constitution and take a new approach at the district level and allow abolition at the district level, there will be no public schools in the state within five years." The opposition, under State Senator Evans, formed a "Committee of 25," made up almost entirely of Citizens' Councils men, to oppose rewriting the constitution and was soon blanketing the state with anti-Coleman material. A United Press tabulation of how the legislators stood prior to the convening of the legislature showed an even split between the two sides, with 25 uncommitted.

After the legislature was convened, Coleman apparently decided the only way he could win was by insisting even more vehemently that only a new constitution could save Mississippi from integration, despite the fact that his original reason for proposing a new constitution was to improve the state's economic position. Mississippi, he declared to a joint session of the legislature, "stands legally naked and legally defenseless" before the integrationists unless it erased all mention of race from the old constitution and left all segregation policies up to the separate school districts.

Senator Evans immediately retorted that "he is asking for just enough integration to satisfy the NAACP." Cole-

85

man later replied: "Senator Evans has called me an integrationist before . . . I am not an integrationist. But if we ever have integration in Mississippi it will be due to men like Senator Evans whose mental processes are so blocked they can't see the necessity of change."

Certainly the "Old Guard" did not see such a necessity, particularly since included in it was a Coleman-approved plan for legislative reapportionment. Many of the "Old Guard" also felt that the constitutional revision was merely a steppingstone for Coleman toward his eventual try to unseat Senator Eastland, while others honestly felt that the best way to alter the constitution was by amendment rather than by a wholesale alteration of a document which had served since 1890.

In any case, in the showdown vote in the House of Representatives the "Old Guard" had the votes, 78–61, and Governor Coleman had received his first major setback since entering politics. Although he promised that "this is only the beginning of the fight—this is chapter one in a very important book," it seemed obvious to most observers that so long as the "Old Guard" faction controlled the legislature, no new constitution would be forthcoming. In the voting it had been the Delta representatives who had formed the core of the opposition to Coleman, and it might be noted that this bloc of representatives had the largest number of Citizens' Council members in the legislature. In 1958 more was to be heard in the legislature from some of these same Citizens' Council supporters.

The special session of the legislature was adjourned shortly after the defeat of the plan for a constitutional convention, and its members went home to a short vacation before the regular session was convened in January 1958. Upon reconvening, the legislature spent nearly three months debating the ways and means of financing a "quality education" bill, finally settling on a measure in early March which could muster enough votes among the "Old Guard" to pass. This bill, which authorized about 98 million dollars for raising teachers' pay and providing funds for nine-month school terms in those districts desiring them, brought the level of teachers' pay in Mississippi up to that of the second lowest paying state, Kentucky, and wiped out whatever differences there had been in salaries paid to equally trained Negro and white teachers. In the field of higher education the legislature appropriated 18 million dollars to raise college instructors' pay almost 20 per cent and to keep the state's Negro colleges on the accredited list. The Citizens' Council kept an official silence on this, nor did any of its officials later lay a claim to its success.

Governor Coleman made one more try for a constitutional convention during this session of the legislature, but, realizing that he still did not have the votes, agreed in a compromise with Walter Sillers to an amendment to the constitution which would make it easier to amend that document. This amendment passed both houses with little dissension and was readied for presentation to the voters of the state in the Democratic primary in August.

Otherwise, a handful of highly controversial measures managed to occupy the legislature's attention so thoroughly that only a few other major pieces of legislation were passed, these being primarily bills designed to buttress further the state's set of "massive resistance" laws. The first of the controversial bills was one providing for a full-scale reapportionment of the legislature, long a smoldering sore point in Mississippi politics because of the radical shifts in population since the original apportionment of legislators had taken place in 1890. Despite the presence of a compromise measure agreed to by Coleman and Walter Sillers, the only results of an interminable amount of debate and committee hearing in both houses were some minor changes in the distribution of seats in a few counties and the method of electing state representatives which satisfied no one and changed very little in the actual balance of power in either house.

A measure which came much closer to passage was one which affected the Citizens' Council directly. It first appeared in the State Senate early in the legislative session under the sponsorship of Senator Hayden Campbell, an active member of the Jackson Citizens' Council. As originally framed and presented to the Senate, it provided that counties or cities could appropriate funds to "any association or organization having as its purpose the perpetuation and preservation of constitutional government and the division of powers thereunder." Senator Campbell explained that it was intended for the Citizens' Councils, although "the Councils did not ask me to introduce this bill. . . . Without them, Mississippi would have lawlessness in its racial relations. The Councils have stood for lawful means of segregation." The senator also made the observation that he thought the State Sovereignty Commission should turn its appropriation over to the Councils since "it hasn't done anything." The bill was then referred to the Judiciary Committee, where the amount which would be allocated for such a purpose was trimmed from $100 per million assessed valuation to 10 per million.

The *Delta Democrat-Times* noted editorially at the time that the bill raised certain assumptions:

1. The Citizens' Councils need dough. 2. Hayden Campbell needs the services of a good psychiatrist. 3. Mississippi's cities and counties need all the tax money they can gather for presently authorized public services. 4. [Should local officials approve such funds their communities] would need new officials. 5. Any objecting taxpayer would need only the services of a capable lawyer to throw the whole mess into the legislative garbage pail where it belongs.

A few weeks later, in early March, a furor over purported "integrationist" activity at Jackson's Millsaps College plus the filing of a suit by the NAACP alleging voting violations against a Negro minister, both of which will be examined in a later chapter, spurred the Senate to sudden activity. The proposed appropriation was raised to $100 per million valuation again, put on the top of the legislative calendar, and passed with only two dissenting votes, both being by senators who would claim they didn't have time to read the bill. This occurred on March 11, the same day Governor Coleman appeared before the legislature to ask once more for a new state constitution.

In the House of Representatives, however, a handful of legislators stood up to oppose the bill. Representative Joe Wroten of Greenville said of it:

It is a vicious assault upon freedom of the mind. A large majority of our citizens have not chosen to affiliate with or to donate their personal funds to the Citizens' Councils. What the people themselves have chosen not to do would be required of them by this bill with the mailed fist of worldly power. I cannot in good conscience witness in silence the passage of this coercive act, which would shackle the minds of a free people, destroy their democratic rights to differences of opinion and pillage their constitutional freedoms.

Other legislators pointed out that the bill was in all probability unconstitutional and that the money appropriated could be given to almost any organization which had control of the county board of supervisors.

A few days later the Jackson *State-Times* came out against the bill, as did the Tupelo *Journal* and the Greenville *Delta Democrat-Times,* but the Jackson *Daily News* gave a front-page editorial in its support. Nevertheless, after all debate was concluded, the House promptly passed a slightly changed version of the bill, one which stated that county or city officials could "employ" organizations and "co-operate" in educational programs for the promotion of constitutional government, rather than "donate" to such organizations. This change in wording was considered necessary to get around a provision of the state constitution which forbids public funds being given to private organizations.

The Senate moved a little more slowly in approving this revised bill than it had in passing the original. Opposition had begun to build up among certain senators, even among some who were Citizens' Council members. As one of the latter said:

> I am an active member of the Citizens' Council. I was active in its organization and have supported it ever since. The Citizens' Council, a spontaneous movement of citizens . . . is the most noble effort since our fathers fought in defense of those same ideals. To put money into these councils will in time absolutely kill them . . . [the members'] interest will wane as a result of governmental interference.

Others simply referred to it as "a damnable piece of legislation," an example of "letting our prejudices get the better of our common sense," and a "two-edged sword."

No state Council official would comment on the issue. Many of the legislators supporting the bill claimed it was not in fact aimed primarily at aiding the Council. However, one of the bill's Senate sponsors let the word out that it had been written by a prominent member of the Jackson Citizens' Council with the full cognizance of the Council leadership.

Then, after maintaining a policy of no comment on the bill, Governor Coleman told a Senate committee that it was "the first step to disaster" by "arming somebody with

$200,000 to control the government affairs of the state. I am not going to preserve segregation by making a headline war between the races." Coleman further stated that he felt the bill was "aimed at the governor" for "refusing to set fire to everything in the state."

Finally, on April 17, nearly a month since it had first been passed by the Senate, the Senate again passed the bill by a vote of 29–19, this time including some additional features not in the House bill. The new amendments required that the State Sovereignty Commission approve use of all funds, that the beneficiary organizations account to the local government for use of the funds under state audit, and that they use none of the money for political purposes. State Senator Lambert, an opponent of the bill, sought unsuccessfully to add an amendment to spell out that the "White Citizens' Councils" would be the recipients of the funds. He said:

> If the Citizens' Councils or any other group can intimidate you—and several members of this Senate have told me they are afraid to vote against the bill— then they can intimidate the boards of supervisors or the boards of aldermen.

Senator Earl Evans felt the Councils had been treated unfairly in the debate. He said:

> Some people in the borders of this state think they have no right to exist. It is true they have exposed some people who have indicated they favored integration but I challenge any man to show where they took part in any political campaign.

The bill, which had passed despite the governor's threat of a veto, then was sent to a joint House-Senate committee to iron out the differences between the two measures. There, for some reason, the bill died with the adjournment of the legislature in late May. After two months of acrimonious debate its death brought no more than a passing glance in any of the state's newspapers or from *The Citizens' Council.*

Perhaps this lack of notice was due in part to the attention accorded the voting suit filed in March by the Reverend H. D. Darby of Prentiss, a Negro who claimed his civil rights had been violated under the application of the state's voting laws, as altered by the 1954 constitutional amendment. Governor Coleman then appeared before the legislature, as already noted, to ask for a change in the state's voting laws.

The voting bill, which was passed by a unanimous vote of both houses, would have made the registrars clerks of a "quasi court," appointed by and under the jurisdiction of the chancery judges for their districts. This would supposedly make the registrar an "inferior court" not subject to contempt of court in voter registration suits brought by the NAACP. One high-ranking member of the "Old Guard" who supported the bill remarked that "we are really getting frantic, aren't we?"

Governor Coleman, after giving it his tacit approval for weeks, vetoed this bill on the grounds that it was unconstitutional and that such action was properly an executive function. This did not bring the expected uproar, because the anti-administration forces were apparently as convinced as the governor that the measure was unconstitutional.

Among the measures which did pass and the governor did sign were: a bill, obviously aimed at the NAACP, calling for an investigation of any organization operating within the state whose directors had been connected with subversive movements; a bill giving legal assistance to the state attorney general in fighting integration suits; a bill authorizing the governor to close any school threatened with integration; a bill allowing the governor or state parks director to close any state park where integration is ordered by the federal courts; a bill authorizing the legislature to investigate the NAACP (by name); and a bill providing for continuation of the State Sovereignty Commission.

While a number of other "segregation" measures were passed by both houses, these were either killed in the rush to adjourn or were vetoed by Governor Coleman. The legislature, having been in session since January, finally wound up its affairs the last week in April and adjourned.

The Citizens' Councils' public activity during this period, other than that which will be noted later, was confined to further exploitation of the public outrage over the Little Rock situation. Its approach to membership solicitation after this event can be illustrated by a quotation from *The Citizens' Council* of April 1958: "If you realize that either Communistic influence or economic pressure groups stand behind every effort to invade States' Rights and force integration and miscegenation on the people of the South, join the Citizens' Council."

Later, in the *Fourth Annual Report,* July 1958, Robert Patterson wrote:

The greatest encounter between the constitutional rights of the people and the states vs. the usurped powers by the Federal Government occurred at Little Rock. "Remember Little Rock" is the battle cry for people who believe it is their sacred right to educate their children in their own way without interference from politically motivated federal sources who know little of local conditions. Because of what happened in Little Rock, Americans everywhere were made aware of the vicious determination of the so-called "liberal minority groups" in their obsession to force their will upon those who differ.

Concerning politics and the Citizens' Council, he wrote:

The Citizens' Council is not a political organization, but in our form of government it is natural that sentiment in favor of racial separation will express itself politically by one method or another. This is already evident in the South, and will be evident in Northern and Western areas eventually.

In the same report the state finance chairman for the Council disclosed that despite the Little Rock uproar there had been little appreciable gain in membership. He said:

I wish I could tell you that we have a big cash balance, that our membership has doubled or even tripled. I cannot make any such statement.

It is to be expected that our people would be apathetic because, I suppose, they feel there is nothing going on that needs attention and that we have nothing to worry about here in Mississippi. This may or may not be true.

The Citizens' Council did not take a discernible part in the Democratic primary in August in which the constitutional amendment providing for easier amending of the constitution passed by a three to one margin. Otherwise the major candidates, including United States Senator John Stennis, were either unopposed or easily defeated their opponents. During the same month the Citizens' Councils of America convened and elected Roy V. Harris of Georgia as president of the association to succeed State Senator W. M. Rainach of Louisiana and re-elected Robert Patterson as executive secretary. The session concerned itself primarily with a review of the Councils' work to date and a discussion of what future action should be taken in the light of the civil rights legislation of the previous fall and the Little Rock school crisis. At the same meeting the newly formed Association of Citizens' Councils of Virginia was admitted to the group.

In September the Citizens' Council of Mississippi sponsored a meeting in Jackson of what *The Citizens' Council* referred to as "prominent businessmen" to hear Republican Representative Ralph W. Gwinn of New York blast the federal government for all aspects of its "creeping socialism," including enforced desegregation. In introducing him, Senator Eastland said, "When you know the people of all sections of the nation, you find that we are not far apart. Segregation is only one feature of the great battle on the American domestic front."

The Citizens' Council wrote:

Veteran observers described the event as the largest of its kind ever held in Jackson, with all those in attendance being top-level business and professional leaders in their own communities. Council leaders are hopeful that similar gatherings may be held throughout the South in the future.

In its same October issue *The Citizens' Council* plugged hard for another of its projects concerning Little Rock. In a black-bordered box on the front page, the paper said:

Contributions to Little Rock should be mailed to Private School Corporation, First National Bank, Little Rock, Arkansas.

If every white person in Mississippi would send $1, the Little Rock private school would have one million dollars.

If every white person in South sent $1, the Little Rock private schools would have 25 million dollars.

Have you sent your dollar?

Within a month a number of local Citizens' Councils were able to answer that question in the affirmative. *The Citizens' Council* noted that the Holmes County Citizens' Council was sponsoring a "Dollars for Little Rock" campaign with the local banks accepting contributions. It was also able to report that the Jefferson County Citizens'

Council had sent $412 to Governor Faubus for the private schools. Other Citizens' Councils throughout the state announced similar intentions or actions during the next two months. Robert Patterson, speaking to a Lions Club meeting in Leland, was moved to say that the Little Rock school crisis was "the finest thing that has yet happened," and that it had given the South a battle cry in "Remember Little Rock" to rival "Remember the Alamo" or "Remember Pearl Harbor."

Meanwhile, Chairman Paul Butler of the Democratic National Committee uttered the first in a series of statements designed to point the way out of the national party for those who did not support the Supreme Court's desegregation decision. Mississippi had been a leader in the States' Rights walkout of the Democratic party in 1948. Now rumblings of rebellion were heard again. When Speaker of the House Sam Rayburn visited Mississippi in early October and refused to comment on the civil rights issue, the loudest applause at the gathering he addressed went to State Democratic Executive Committee Chairman Bidwell Adam, old-time political opponent of Governor Coleman's, who said:

I want to tell the honorable speaker that I am not a milk chocolate Democrat. I am an old line Democrat who is not even about to drink the dregs left by "Soapy" Williams or any other liberal. I am tired of furnishing a back for them to practice their bull whip lessons on.

Ten days later Butler's well-publicized remark that opponents of a strong civil rights plank "will have to go their own way" added to Mississippi's political unrest. John Bell Williams referred to the "betrayal" of the South within the party, and Bidwell Adam said that Butler was "trying to drive the South out of the party." Governor Coleman, in a major departure from his efforts to keep Mississippi Democrats loyal to the national party, warned:

The end result [of a third party] would be to isolate us from both major parties, leave us no powerful friends anywhere, and thus allow us to be destroyed at the convenience of our adversaries. At the same time, I realize that things could be done in 1960 that would not leave us any other honorable course. . . . But if it cannot be avoided, then we shall simply have to face up to the unavoidable and leave ourselves to whatever fate may have in store for us.

Governor Coleman himself had met strong criticism two weeks earlier for accepting his election as chairman of the Southern Governors' Conference in place of Governor Faubus of Arkansas, and his sincerity was suspected by those who were seriously planning to bolt the party. Judge Brady roundly denounced the governor in a speech to the Jackson Lions Club which many thought was the forerunner of an expected announcement—which never was made—of his candidacy for governor in 1960. Labeling Coleman a "moderate," Brady said:

I was sorely struck when our Governor issued a statement that he was greatly honored to be elected Chairman of the Southern Governors' Conference over a man rightfully earning that position.

The picture of Governor Orval E. Faubus of Arkansas, a great fighter for our way of life, being bypassed for our own Governor, who should have been the first to stand up and defend him, troubles me.

Can't you just see men like Faubus and Marvin Griffin of Georgia sitting across the table hearing such scalawags as Clement of Tennessee, Collins of Florida, that integrationist Happy Chandler of Kentucky and Republican Theodore McKeldin applauding our Governor of the most segregated state in the Union?

How fine a thing, had our Governor stood up and told the world that this state and himself stand solidly back of Governor Faubus and Governor Almond of Virginia. What a wonderful opportunity he had to rise and refuse to accept the nomination over the man entitled to it, Arkansas' Faubus. How proud we could have been of him, had he done that instead of boasting that he was honored as a moderate. We are ashamed that our leadership in Mississippi is unable to speak out in defense of us.

The national elections in November did little to improve either Coleman's position in the eyes of the Citizens' Council leadership as personified by Brady or the mood of many state Democrats about association with the national party. The latter feeling could be expected with the sweep by the Northern liberals and the omens for future civil rights action it presaged, but the further undermining of Coleman's position in the eyes of the

Citizens' Council adherents and "Old Guarders" was a little more involved.

The background for this was provided a few days before the national election, when Representative Brooks Hays of Arkansas, faced by the threat of a write-in segregationist candidate who was attacking him for his moderation, telephoned Governor Coleman and asked him to make a statement endorsing him as a loyal Southerner. Hays evidently considered this necessary since Governor Faubus was working behind the scenes for his opponent. Influenced by the help Hays had given him in working out a compromise plank on civil rights at the national convention in Chicago in 1956, Governor Coleman agreed.

In a tape-recorded telephone conversation, Coleman described Hays as "true to the traditions of the South and to the traditions of Arkansas and Mississippi" and continued: "The South needs you in her great struggle . . ." He recalled Hays's defense of the South's position at the 1956 Democratic convention and said that Arkansas voters would be surrendering to "eleventh hour hysteria" if they elected Dr. Dale Alford, a Little Rock school board member and the write-in candidate. The night before the election Hays appeared on the Little Rock television stations in a paid political appearance and played the recording. But the next day the effort seemed to have gone for nothing as he lost in a close race to Dr. Alford.

In Mississippi an immediate storm of controversy arose over Governor Coleman's "interference" in the politics of another state, particularly since he had been so careful to avoid any mention of the Arkansas situation before. *The Citizens' Council* carried a long editorial happily describing Hays's fall from power and inserting the hope that all moderates would soon follow him. In immediate reply Governor Coleman commented: "Regardless of these critics who are working day and night to stir up trouble, I have no apology to make for telling the truth about Brooks Hays."

The critical comment, more and more directed at Governor Coleman for his "moderation" and his support of the national party, continued. Judge Brady, sounding more and more like a candidate for governor, insinuated to one Jackson audience, as a writer for the United Press put it, "that the Governor is in league with integrationists and has refused to oppose left-wing elements of the Democratic party in order to advance his chances for a national office." Brady further charged that Coleman had allowed "integrationist" textbooks in the public schools. One such book was *Adventures for Readers Book I,* which the judge said contained an article "calculated to obliterate from the minds of our boys and girls any racial differences which actually exist between the white and Negro races in this country."

In a later speech to the Madison County Citizens' Council, Brady insisted that the schools remained segregated "not because of the work of one person as that one person so often claims, but because of the courageous men in the legislature and you who decided our schools would be abolished before we would integrate." Referring to Coleman as "Fair-minded Jim," Brady charged that he was in league with Adlai Stevenson and Harry Truman (an old Mississippi bugaboo) because all three had given support to Brooks Hays. The tenor of his speech was also indicated by his reference to Sam Rayburn as "that eggheaded man from Texas who is arch-traitor to the South."

Governor Coleman blasted back at the "calamity howlers" who wished "to toss matches into gasoline barrels." He said that there are "a few politicians who are keenly disappointed that the Coleman administration has handled the school situation with complete success. They publicly pretend that they are great believers in the separation of the races, but they secretly pray for trouble in order to discredit us."

The year drew to a close on two more notes which provided some hint as to the future course of politics in Mississippi. The first was the announcement by Judge Brady that he would run for governor "if the people of Mississippi want me to," but that his decision would rest on an informal survey he was making to "keep from being a fool" in running without popular support.

The other was the formation of a steering committee for a States' Rights party in Mississippi. Headed by Circuit Judge M. M. McGowan of Jackson, an active Citizens' Council member, the committee had as its immediate aim the creation of States' Rights committees in each county. In explaining its purpose Judge McGowan said:

We are sliding helplessly into a one party system in America . . . that means a socialist government.

The master minds of socialism who control both major parties do not care which one wins. But the very thought of throwing the election into the House strikes terror in their hearts.

The heel of tyranny has temporarily shifted from Arkansas to Alabama. Where the Lyndon Johnson-Sam Rayburn "Civil Rights Compromise" is reaping its harvest of despotism and oppression . . . compromises are our most deadly enemies.

Bidwell Adam, the Democratic State Executive Committee chairman, said of Judge McGowan:

He and I see eye to eye on a lot of issues. We are all interested in absolute preservation of segregation. That's the only comment I can make on the States' Righters at this time.

However, I may have to cut one ear off the donkey if Paul Butler doesn't put a piece of tape across his mouth.

William Simmons declared in January 1959 that any support of a third party would "depend entirely on the events of the next two years. It is an open question until then." But it is interesting to note, particularly in view of the activities of the Citizens' Council before and during the state Democratic convention of 1956, what Judge Brady wrote in *Black Monday* on the subject of a third party:

The Nationalist Federation of Sovereign States [his suggested name for what later took form in the Citizens' Council], if necessary, can be converted in a third National Party since two major parties, in fact or in principle, do not exist in the United States today.

The matter rested there as 1958 ended. The first four years of existence has seen the Mississippi Citizens' Council expand from a handful of men in the Delta to a group estimated at 85,000, toward which most of the state's politicians made frequent bows and whose members, if not the organization itself, were actively engaged in politics and indeed were playing leading roles. This position of prominence rested on more than politics or political action, however, and it is with these other bases that the next two chapters are concerned.

CHAPTER IV

The Citizens' Councils and the Negro

As a race the Negro is definitely inferior to the white.
The only fields in which they are superior are in their
physical strength and their natural capacity as enter-
tainers, making fun of themselves for the benefit of
others.

Robert Patterson

If you have had a negro mammy take care of you and
keep you from eating dirt; if you played with negro
boys when a boy; if you have worked with and among
them, laughed at their ribald humor; if you have been
stunned by their abysmal vulgarity and profanity; if you
can find it in your heart to overlook their obscenity and
depravity; if you can respect and love their deep religious
fervor; if you can cherish and love their loyalty and de-
votion to you, then you are beginning to understand the
negro.

Judge Tom P. Brady, *Black Monday*

107

ANY PRESENTATION of the relationship between the Citizens' Council and pressures directed at the Negro race within Mississippi must first start with two basic premises. The first is that the majority of whites sincerely believe, and have believed, that basically the Negro is inferior to the Caucasian race. An army of sociologists and historians have attempted to destroy this belief, but it still remains.

The second is that unpunished violence of white against black is not a result primarily of the events and pressures of the past four years but has been a part of Mississippi's heritage since Reconstruction. No single organized group of whites can take either the credit or the blame for much of the violence and pressure which the Mississippi Negro has experienced since the Supreme Court decision of 1954. It has simply been, in large measure, the natural result of Mississippi's mainstream of race relations over the past ninety years.

It must then also be stated that there is strong evidence to support the proposition that the inherent feelings of most white Mississippians on the race question have been aroused and channelized by the activities of the Citizens' Council since its inception. In any case, one method the Citizens' Councils were often accused of using in their drive to their present position was the physical, economic, and psychological intimidation of Negroes who "didn't know their place." How true this charge is in its entirety will be examined later, but it is certain that activity directed either against individual Negroes or against organized groups of that race was advocated by Council leaders in Mississippi early in the organization's formation.

Economic pressure against Negro and white opponents of the Citizens' Council and its aims was first advocated by one of the original founders of the movement, Arthur Clark, the Indianola attorney whose tape-recorded suggestions in 1954 have already been reviewed. According to the magazine, *New South,* a publication of the Southern Regional Council—itself a target of the Councils—he also said at that time:

It is the thought of our group that the solution of this problem may become easier if various agitators and the like could be removed from the communities in which they now operate. We propose to accomplish this through the careful application of economic pressure upon those men who cannot be controlled otherwise. If the proper organization is perfected and proper liaison had between all elements, the medium of economic pressure can be used quite effectively to the end that those who stir up discontent may be removed from the community.

Another of the original leaders of the Council, Fred Jones, of Inverness, a former state legislator and now a member of the State Executive Committee of the Citizens' Council, was quoted in several newspaper stories as saying in October 1954:

We can accomplish our purposes largely with economic pressure in dealing with members of the Negro race who are not cooperating, and with members of the white race who fail to cooperate, we can apply social and political pressure.

Later, during an organizational meeting of a Citizens' Council held outside the state of Mississippi (in Dallas County, Alabama) which was addressed by several members of the Mississippi Council, one speaker said:

> We intend to make it difficult, if not impossible, for any Negro who advocates desegregation to find and hold a job, get credit, or renew a mortgage.

Nevertheless, many Council leaders today are emphatic in their denial of the advocacy or use of economic pressure by the Citizens' Councils at any time. Their denials have been repeated many times and in many different ways. Some of them follow. Thomas Waring, a Charleston, South Carolina, newspaper editor, wrote in the first issue of *The Citizens' Council:*

> "Economic pressure," a method of combatting Negro pressure from the North, is not organized by the Councils. Individuals who belong to Councils may have persuaded Negroes to remove their names from school integration petitions by various means short of violence. These means could include firing employees, or refusing to renew leases for share croppers who have followed the NAACP line.

> If these tactics have been used—and there seems little doubt that they have—they were adopted on individual initiative and not as a group action.

Robert Patterson was quoted in another source as saying:

The Association of Citizens' Councils of Mississippi has never advocated economic pressure. Of course, we don't denounce individuals who use freedom of choice in their business arrangement. . . . The only boycott we have heard of lately is that used by the NAACP, the CIO, and our Federal government. . . . This is the dagger, the cannon, and the atomic bomb of the mongrelizers. Must we use peeled bananas, water pistols, and cream puffs against these weapons?

Judge Brady, who had advocated economic pressure against the Negro as a last resort in his book, *Black Monday,* had another view on it in 1957. He said:

There never has been any organized economic pressure that I know of by the Councils. It's a terrible thing, a horrible thing to use and it can cut and hurt deep . . . But it is interesting to note how the unions and the NAACP protest when they've been using the same weapon for years.

William Simmons, another member of the State Executive Committee and the editor of *The Citizens' Council,* also said in 1957:

No, there never has been any economic pressure by the Councils as such. There never has been any organized attempt or recommendations to that effect by any Council. . . . As for economic pressure on Negroes themselves, when the petition for integrated schools was presented here in Jackson by 43 Negroes, all of them lost their jobs except those in public employ, but to my knowledge only one of their employers was a Citizens' Council member.

When people are annoyed by anything you can just expect them to react against the source of their annoyance. So it is with Niggers who persist in acting against what their employers think is correct.

Despite these denials today, there were many among both Negroes and whites in 1954 and 1955 who thought that they had definite proof of pressure being directed against the Negroes by the Citizens' Council. In Mississippi itself one or two newspapers kept up a steady stream of criticism of this aspect of Citizens' Council activity. Elsewhere, men who could be put in neither the moderate nor the liberal camp on the segregation question protested against the tactics of the Council. One writer, W. E. Debnam, whose book otherwise was an attack upon "Yankee interference" in the South's problems, said:

> The Citizens' Council idea is to make the Supreme Court's decision null and void in Mississippi by stopping all moves on the part of any Negro looking toward taking advantage of that decision. It's a let-it-wither-on-the-vine technique to be accomplished by the bringing to bear of economic pressure.
>
> It's a blow below the belt . . . and the South demeans itself when it resorts to any such tactics. It's a dangerous thing that smacks of the tactics of a Hitler or a Stalin. . . . We can lick this Thing without resorting to such tactics.

Another voice heard in opposition to the Council was the Montgomery, Alabama, *Advertiser,* which carried an editorial on November 30, 1954, which said:

The stated aims of the White Citizens' Councils is to throttle free speech and impose thought control by means of an economic claw. . . . What is proposed is indecent and vicious because we find a dominant group standing in the shadows threatening to confiscate the meat, drink, and shelters of dissenters.

Incidentally, both the Montgomery *Advertiser* and Debnam later changed their minds and became Citizens' Council supporters. The stated reasons for their change of heart boiled down to the idea that they were misinformed in their original opposition as to the full nature of the Councils.

Soon thereafter, the Negro organizations attempted a counter-attack against the forces which they felt were exerting pressures on their race in Mississippi. On January 9, 1955, the NAACP announced that it was inaugurating a drive to raise money to meet the asserted economic assaults of pressure by the Councils in Mississippi, and on January 20, affidavits alleging instances of such pressure were filed with the White House.

An earlier announcement by Mississippi's then Attorney General Coleman that the number of Negro voters in January was down to 12,000 from an estimated 22,000 in 1952 spurred activity by another Negro group. The Mississippi Regional Council of Negro Leadership announced in mid-January that it was attempting to raise $100,000 to test the legality of the recently passed voting amendment. In a statement released to the press, a spokesman for the Regional Council said that the amendment and Citizens' Councils activity were directly responsible for the sharp drop in Negro voting. No voting suit materialized, however.

Throughout 1955 there were to be more and more reports of alleged Citizens' Council pressure directed against Negroes, and more and more proven instances of such pressure being used by whites, whether Council members or not. On March 17, 1955, the NAACP charged that Gus Courts, a Negro grocer in Belzoni, had been forced by the Citizens' Council to vacate his building after he refused to withdraw his name from the voter registration rolls. However, C. L. Puckett, the secretary of the Humphreys County Citizens' Council (Belzoni is in Humphreys County), was quoted as saying that the council was not involved, and that the eviction was ordered only because the grocer, Gus Courts, "wasn't paying his rent regularly."

Courts disagreed with Puckett. He said that he had been forced out of the building because of his determination to vote, something he had never done in his life. After he was evicted, he said, he was shown a list of the county's 95 Negroes who were still on the vote rolls and told that they were all going to lose their jobs just as he had lost his store if they didn't withdraw their names. According to him, the president of Belzoni's Guaranty Bank and Trust, claiming to speak for the Citizens' Council, warned that "if you don't back down, we'll force you out of business."

Ten days later, on March 27, the *Delta Democrat-Times* carried a front-page story under the title, "There's a List in Belzoni." It stated that the Citizens' Council in Humphreys County was circulating a list of the registered Negro voters still left on the rolls, and that those whose names appeared thereon were being fired from their jobs, denied credit, or intimidated in other ways. It noted that the 95 who were named on the petition were the only Negro voters in a total Negro population of 16,000 in the county.

The NAACP increased its efforts to find some way to combat this situation. On April 9, 1955, NAACP Executive Secretary Roy Wilkins announced that "the tide had been turned." He said that a quarter of a million dollars given by various Negro organizations and some labor unions had been deposited in a Memphis Negro bank to be used specifically by Negroes caught in the Citizens' Council sponsored economic pinch. How effective this money actually was is hard to determine, though it is known that several Negroes were beneficiaries. Certainly, however, little was written about it thereafter.

Belzoni returned to the headlines a little later. On May 8, 1955, the Reverend George Lee, a Negro minister in Belzoni, who had been one of the first to qualify as a voter and had recently led the Negro registration drive, was shot to death while driving his car in the Negro section of Belzoni.

The local sheriff and other law enforcement officers took ten days to determine the cause of death, there being some inclination at first to believe that the particles found in his mouth and face were fillings from his teeth and not lead from a bullet. Finally an FBI laboratory report settled the matter in favor of the bullet, and the NAACP promptly charged that Lee had been shot because of his voting activity. Sheriff Ike Shelton of Belzoni said that this was "absurd," and that Lee had actually been shot by another Negro in an argument over a woman.

A coroner's jury returned a verdict of death by "causes unknown," and the NAACP immediately called for a mass protest meeting to be held in Belzoni under the protection of the FBI. Such protection was necessary, the NAACP said, since the "advent of the Citizens' Councils had made local law enforcement break down." In the course of the uneventful mass meeting, which was held without FBI protection, Dr. McCoy, state NAACP president, said, "I directly blame the Citizens' Council for Lee's murder," although Roy Wilkins, who also attended the meeting, would not go as far as this, being content to blame it upon the white community in general.

C. L. Puckett again denied all such charges. He was certain, he said, that no Citizens' Council member had committed the murder, since "violence is against our constitution and by-laws." It didn't matter to him, Puckett said, whether the murderer was a white man or a Negro. In either case the man should be convicted. Judge Brady later said that he went to Belzoni to investigate the causes of the murder and that Puckett "swore to God that it was no white man who shot Lee, but another Negro." However, despite the stated aim of all interested parties, no one has ever been brought to trial for this crime.

While violence might have been against the Humphreys

County Citizens' Council's bylaws and constitution, apparently a little non-violent pressure was not. The United Press carried a story on May 19, the same day the coroner's jury returned its verdict, which was concerned with a form letter circulated around Humphreys County under a Citizens' Council masthead. The letter said:

> It is our understanding that a number of farmers of this county are dissatisfied with services their tenants have received from local undertakers. As a public service, the Humphreys County Citizens' Council has checked Negro undertakers of adjoining counties and have found two in Indianola that meet our standards.

These "standards" were not disclosed, but a probable cause of the farmers "dissatisfaction" was that the only Negro undertaker in Belzoni, T. V. Johnson, was a member of the NAACP. What effect this letter had upon Johnson's business is uncertain, but NAACP membership in Belzoni dropped off sharply within a few weeks.

The summer of 1955 saw the gubernatorial compaign mentioned earlier. In such a race in Mississippi, the Negro "problem" is usually issue number one. Certainly none of the candidates solicited the Negro vote, and in some cases there were definite efforts made to see that this vote, unsolicited or otherwise, was not cast. United Press correspondent John Herbers noted that the Negroes "may not want to vote for lack of a friend among the candidates. And they may be afraid to vote in areas where the Citizens' Councils have been active."

The white community of the state was in no mood for

any kind of Negro activity after the NAACP filed desegregation petitions, all of which were rejected or ignored,
with the Vicksburg, Clarksdale, Natchez, Jackson, and
Yazoo City school boards. There was an immediate heated
reaction to these petitions, as already noted, with all of the
candidates attacking them. Within a few days after the
petitions were filed in each city, Negroes began "volun-
tarily" requesting that their names be removed. Some
claimed that their signatures were forgeries, while others
simply had them removed with no comment. By September the petitions were withdrawn for lack of support.

However, there was comment from some quarters in the
state concerning alleged activity by the Citizens' Council
in removing Negro voters from the rolls. What was left
of the original 95 Negro voters in Humphreys County
petitioned the governor for protection on the coming election day, complaining again of Citizens' Council economic
pressure. Governor White refused to authorize any protection, and when Gus Courts led 22 Negroes to the polls in
the first primary, all of them were challenged and their
ballots voided.

In the meantime, Robert Patterson had issued a statement for the Citizens' Council saying that it was "not
opposed" to Negro voting, a statement which led one
optimistic Negro editor in Jackson to suggest that the
Citizens' Councils should themselves patrol the polls and
protect any Negroes who might vote. "Mr. Patterson war-
rants the hearty thanks and congratulations from all intelligent Negroes of the state for his statement," he said.

As it turned out, the State Democratic Committee or lo-

118

cal registrars took care of most of those Negroes who did try to vote, and the question of Citizens' Council "protection" or repression was not a matter of great importance in the election. The election did bring another sensational act of violence against a Negro, however, again apparently for election activities. On August 13, 1955, Lemar Smith, a Negro who, according to the local district attorney, had been "messing around" as an active supporter for one of the candidates in the Pike County supervisor's race was shot down at midday in front of the courthouse. Despite the time of day and the fact that there were a number of people in the immediate vicinity, the three white men who were indicted have never been brought to trial. Incidentally, Judge Brady is the circuit judge for that district, and he has said that he thought the reason no trial has been held is that no white man is willing to testify against another in the murder of a Negro. No witnesses would come forward to testify to the grand juries, the judge adds, and he could only charge them on the basis of the slight evidence obtained at the time by the district attorney.

There was no connection between the Citizens' Council and this shooting, but the state's Negroes could not help but see some link between the unpunished slayings and the victims' desire to vote.

The Smith killing was scarcely off the front pages of the state's newspapers when the Emmett Till murder in the last week of August rocked the state once more. The first indication of what was to come appeared in a small United Press story from Greenwood, which said that a local storekeeper had been charged with abducting a Negro youth. This was on August 29. The next day a more detailed story was sent out recounting that two men had been charged with kidnaping. Then, on August 31 the inevitable headlines appeared: "Kidnapped Youth Found Slain Near Greenwood."

Almost immediately Robert Patterson issued a statement calling the killing "regrettable" and denying that it could be attributed to the Citizens' Council. "This is absolutely not so," he said, "no more than the boy's death can be attributed to the church he belonged to." The Council was thereafter to play little public part in the Till trial, and there were few charges that it was either responsible for the murder or for the verdicts of not guilty which were returned against the two men indicted. The criticisms of Mississippi during and after the two trials were blanket indictments of the whole state, not selective attacks upon any special target within its borders. One exception to this was a formal petition filed with the Justice Department by the NAACP which called upon the government to halt immediately the "state of jungle fury" in Mississippi, the "atmosphere of violence" which had been instilled by the Citizens' Councils and which had led to the deaths of Till, the Reverend Lee, and Lemar Smith.

It is noteworthy in respect to the trial which followed the murder that Governor-elect Coleman sent his own special agent, a former FBI man, to help the prosecution wherever he could. Despite such assistance, however, a community and jury, obviously aroused by "outside interference," freed both men on trial for the murder.

This "atmosphere of violence" produced two more publicized shootings of Negroes by whites in Mississippi during the latter part of 1955. Gus Courts, the Belzoni grocer, was shot and critically wounded in his newly located store on the evening of November 25. Badly hurt as he was, he nevertheless ordered his friends to take him to the hospital in the all-Negro town of Mound Bayou, some 75 miles' distance from Belzoni. This flight annoyed Sheriff Shelton, who felt that it impeded the progress of his investigation, but he did come up with a theory soon thereafter that the assailant was a "light-skinned Negro man," despite the later testimony of both Courts and the only eyewitness that he had been a white man.

The eyewitness, Mrs. Savannah Luton, refused to change her story, and later claimed that she was taken off the relief rolls immediately after testifying at the inquiry. Courts moved to Chicago soon after recovering from his wounds, his departure having some of the overtones of the working of the "Underground Railroad" of pre-Civil War days.

The next killing, like the others, went unpunished. In December, Elmer Kimbrell, a white man and good friend of the two men charged with Till's death, shot a Negro filling-station attendant, Roy Melton of Glendora, Mississippi, in full sight of the white service-station owner. The next month a trial jury found the killing justified as "self-defense," despite the fact that neither the sheriff nor the station owner could find the gun Melton was alleged to have pulled on Kimbrell. With this slaying and subsequent trial, the state ended 1955 and began 1956 with a record of four shootings of Negroes by whites and no convictions, a score which undoubtedly gave pause to any Negroes bent on asserting their "rights" in any field.

During the summer and fall of 1955, the Citizens' Councils were reported to be hard at work themselves in less violent pursuits. For instance, according to one source, the Jackson Citizens' Council began using a mimeographed "confidential communiqué" to spread the word to all members. "Confidential Communiqué Number 14," sent out on August 22, 1955, made a point of listing the activities of an unsavory Negro integrationist, Arrington High. Within a week after this bill of particulars was distributed, he was asked to withdraw his money from the bank and his home was being subjected to increasing vandalism. Again there is no provable connection between the circular and the subsequent events, since the letter made no mention of what action should be taken against High and others, but the coincidence was enough to convince High that the Council was responsible.

Another example of this type of Citizens' Council activity came after the filing of the Yazoo City school desegregation petition. The Yazoo City Citizens' Council sponsored an advertisement in the local paper which gave the names of the petition's signers and advised the reader to "look them over carefully." By August, 35 of the original 53 who signed the petition had asked to have their names removed, and by September there were only six names left. Again the Council could and did claim that it was not responsible for whatever forced or persuaded the signers to withdraw their names, and again there is no provable connection between the two events. Nevertheless, it seems obvious that the two had some relationship.

There were enough such examples for Oliver Emmerich, editor of the McComb *Enterprise-Journal,* to write an editorial in August calling for co-operation between the races rather than intimidation. He said:

The extent to which the people of Mississippi are able to maintain segregated schools depends upon the good will and cooperation which exists between the leadership of the two races. The great masses of white and Negro people can find a common ground upon which to meet—the idea of good schools, separate but equal—for the two races maintained out of a sense of good will and not because of threats or intimidations.

While it might be doubted that these words were heeded by those interested in the use of "threats or intimidation" in the solution of Mississippi's racial problem, they did presage a three-year period in which overt physical violence against the Negro virtually disappeared from Mississippi, those incidents that did occur being unrelated to the Negro's quest for fuller rights. The use of economic pressure did not vanish, however, nor did political activity intended to curb the Negro's use of the ballot. The NAACP came under mounting fire also in the next three years, the white community being in full agreement that, without the power of that organization in the councils of "the North," the desegregation controversy would never have come to a head.

Reports of pressure against individual Negroes continued to crop up periodically, February of 1956 being an indicative month. Two Negro women claimed early that month that they had been discharged from the Coahoma County Hospital because their names were on the school desegregation petition of the month before. Later in the same month Dr. T. R. M. Howard, founder of the Regional Council of Negro Leadership, announced that he was mailing a check for $5000 to R. L. Drew of Clarksdale, the local NAACP president, to help him meet the alleged economic pressure of the Citizens' Council.

Howard, a prosperous physician, reported that he was going to sell most of his private holdings because of Council pressure. He had played a very prominent role in the side show attendant upon the Till trial, issuing public statements designed to infuriate most white Mississippians and generally playing shepherd to the host of out-of-state Negroes who flocked into Mississippi to attend the trial as spectators and reporters. Soon thereafter he quit the state, although maintaining a legal residence there, and embarked on a series of lectures denouncing segregation, Mississippi, and the Citizens' Council.

The number of Negro voters was cut back drastically in the national election of 1956, many being frightened out of attempting to vote by the shooting of Courts and Lee in 1955, others being eliminated by the state's new voting requirements. Out of the 22,000 reported Negro voters in 1952, only 8000 were left to make the attempt in 1956, and most of these were restricted to the larger towns. In most rural counties, where the majority of Mississippi's 985,000 Negroes live, not one Negro voter even bothered to try to vote. In many of those areas where they did attempt to vote, they were turned away with no explanation given.

Actually, on the surface 1956 was an extremely calm year in Mississippi insofar as race relations were concerned. The state government had stepped out forcefully in its regular session early in the year to erect a barricade of "massive resistance" laws, and the Citizens' Council was busy consolidating and improving the position it had gained over the past two years. The activity that organization was engaged in vis-à-vis the Negro was more psychological than economic or physical, moreover, and was not the type which would make headlines.

The proposals for a Civil Rights Bill coming from the new Congress moved Governor Coleman to comment to reporters on February 7, 1957, that there was no intimidation of Negroes in Mississippi and that the Civil Rights Bill was an affront to a patriotic section of the country. The next day the field secretary for the NAACP in Mississippi, Medgar Evers, released a statement attacking the governor's reported remarks. Evers' statement said:

> It is true that this bill may be late for Emmit Till of Chicago, Illinois, Lamar Smith of Brookhaven, the Reverend G. W. Lee and Gus Courts of Belzoni, and Roy Melton of Glendora, but it will not be too late for 985,000 Negroes who still live in a state where police

brutality is on the increase. It will not be too late for Negroes in the state who cannot get justice in the courts, and where white people take the law in their own hands. . . .

We deplore the statement that Negroes are not intimidated when teachers had to sign an oath that they were not members of the NAACP. Negroes who seek their civil and human rights are subject to economic reprisals. . . .

One Negro who left the state in 1957 was certain that he could place the blame on the Citizens' Council for the reprisals directed against him for being a militant leader of the Negro community in Indianola, the birthplace of the Council and his home town. He was Dr. Clinton C. Battle, a young doctor who had received his medical degree under the terms of the Mississippi Medical Education Loan Program. Dr. Battle waited until June 1957, the month his five years of practice in Mississippi required by the provisions of the loan were up, and then left, after charging that his patients had been advised by Citizens' Council members not to come to him and that his voting rights had been systematically impaired by Council activity.

He said he had gone to the FBI with one particular instance of irregular procedure by the county registrar in connection with his ballot, "but they sent a man who was born and raised in Mississippi to investigate. He told me I should tell the sheriff. These FBI men aren't going to make charges against their friends and neighbors. When I saw that the federal government wasn't going to do anything about the violation of my civil rights, I decided I may as well move out of the state."

The Indianola NAACP had died because of Council opposition, Battle said, and most Mississippi Negroes were now afraid "to speak out against violations of their voting rights . . ."

The state NAACP wasn't drying up fast enough for some whites in Mississippi, however, a fact which was indicated by a talk Lieutenant Governor Carroll Gartin made in late June on the Citizens' Council Forum, a television program then originating in Jackson. He said that the NAACP would probably be outlawed by the legislature in January 1958. He continued:

> When the legislature meets in January, that will be gone into thoroughly. Some in the legislature with whom I talked favor making the names of members of the NAACP and other like organizations public. Personally, I think a law outlawing the NAACP would have a great effect in this state. Some say it would simply drive them underground but at the same time lots of good law-abiding Mississippi Negroes are being misled into joining the NAACP and if they knew it was illegal those Negroes would not have membership in such an organization. I think it would be a good thing.

The Citizens' Council also thought this action would be a good thing, devoting large sections of *The Citizens' Council* to reports of the NAACP's reported Communist

127

affiliations, of the "front" records of many of its directors, and of its hidden drive for ultimate intermarriage and "mongrelization." Of all the issues which the Council paper was to raise, this was the one it returned to most often over the first three years of its existence.

The NAACP also came under attack in 1957 from a highly unexpected direction. Although there was and is a division in Mississippi between the conservative Negro leadership, which advocates continued segregation and an emphasis on material gains as the Negro's goal, and the more "activist" NAACP leadership which stands for immediate integration, this split rarely spilled over into the state's white newspapers. From time to time *The Citizens' Council* might quote approvingly from some Negro's defense of continued segregation, or even, as in one instance, distribute such a defense in a printed sheet to its membership, but this was about as far as such publicity went.

Then, on March 3, 1957, came the first of a series of eight articles in the Jackson *State-Times*, a white newspaper, written by Clennon King, a Negro professor at Alcorn A & M, a small Negro college. The first sentence of his first article began, "Perhaps the NAACP is the National Association for the Agitation of Colored People after all." The remainder of this article and the following seven included a critical examination of most of the "activists" beliefs and actions.

On March 6 the entire student body of Alcorn A & M walked out in protest against these stories and demanded that King be dismissed before they would return to class.

The State College Board dismissed the college president instead for not keeping the students in line, and the students gradually filtered back to the school, although none returned to King's classes. The state's newspapers happily played up the actions and further statements of this NAACP enemy from within, although there were some private doubts expressed as to his sincerity.

In an ironic sequel to the story, a year later, the doubters were given supporting evidence. After the students returned to Alcorn, King was retained through the 1957–58 term, but he did not teach a single class. He moved to Gulfport, Mississippi, to take the pastorate of a church there after being dismissed from his church in Hazlehurst by a congregation which was not in accord with his controversial stand. Then, at the conclusion of the 1958 school term, his contract was terminated at Alcorn.

In late May 1958, King told his congregation in Gulfport that he was planning to enroll in the University of Mississippi summer school to work toward a doctor's degree in history. He also said that he was a supporter of the NAACP and had always belonged to it. In the furor that followed, King announced that he had four of the five endorsements by school alumni that were needed by any applicant to a state university; and on June 5 he appeared at the University of Mississippi, a segregated institution.

Even if he could have enrolled he could not have worked toward a doctorate in history, since the University does not offer one, but King didn't have time to worry about that. He was met by state officials, who told him his petition for entry was not in order, then whisked him off to Jackson, put him in a secret cell, and held him incommunicado for 24 hours. The next day he was committed to the state insane asylum, but before court proceeding could be inaugurated to free him, he was pronounced sane and released. He then boarded a plane for his home town in Georgia, telling the newsmen who saw him off that "I don't want to stay in Mississippi if I'm not wanted. I haven't been treated right. I'm convinced that whites in authority don't want me."

Three months later King made headlines again by announcing his intention to enroll his daughter in a white elementary school in Gulfport. He was blocked in this by his wife, who took their children back to Georgia and enrolled them in school there, ending for the time being King's attempts to bring about integration in Mississippi.

Another highly vocal Negro integrationist was sent to the state mental hospital in 1958. A considerable number of both white and Negro Mississippians believed that Arrington High, the other Negro, belonged there. High, an old target of the Citizens' Council, was the editor of a newssheet called the *Eagle Eye* and had long been a vociferous critic of most of Mississippi's institutions and leaders. His articles tended to be somewhat incoherent and garbled, and among his own race he was considered to be a little "touched." As the president of the Regional Council of Negro Leadership put it, "High is a highly irrational man. I don't know if he is really insane, but he is eccentric."

At any rate, he seemed eccentric enough to his step-father to have him committed in February 1958, after High threatened to publish the names of the white patrons of a Negro house of prostitution in Jackson. Subsequently, he escaped and turned up in Chicago, where he told the press that he had been smuggled out of Mississippi by an "Underground Railway," hidden in a coffin. All local Negro leaders scoffed at this tale and suggested that it was more probable that he had simply walked away from his minimum security area at the institution and taken a train to Chicago. Whatever the truth, it made a good story, although the Clennon King incident soon surpassed it.

In the meantime the state legislature passed a bill in its regular session in early 1958 authorizing an investigation of the NAACP, although it did not vote to outlaw the organization, and in June the General Legislative Investigating Committee began its probe behind closed doors. Its chairman, State Senator Stanton Hall, said that the probe was "just a watchdog action . . . to keep an eye on them" and it had no definite plans.

Medgar Evers, the NAACP field secretary in Mississippi, said that no NAACP records had been requested by the committee, but that the association welcomed such a probe. He continued:

> In fact, we'd gloat at the opportunity. . . . We condemn other countries that deny freedom of the ballot, but we here in Mississippi, in the so called American way of life, are denied the right to vote. . . . Senator Hall would do well to investigate conditions in his

home county where Americans are denied the rights of citizenship.

The NAACP had already initiated a court test for one Negro "denied the rights of citizenship." Three months earlier, in March, Negro minister H. D. Darby of Prentiss, Mississippi, brought suit in Jackson, charging that he was being denied his constitutional rights by being kept from voting in Jefferson Davis County. His suit, financed by the NAACP, named Circuit Clerk James Daniel and Mississippi Attorney General J. T. Patterson as defendants, and attacked the constitutionality of the state's 1954 voting amendment. Darby stated that he filled out the written examination required by state law in Daniel's office June 22, 1957, but that after he completed it Daniel advised him he could not register because he had not met the state's constitutional requirements for interpreting the constitution or understanding the duties and obligations of citizenship under the constitutional form of government. Darby added he had appealed but that the Board of Election commissioners had never acted on his appeal.

Soon after the suit was filed, Attorney General Patterson warned that this litigation, "if followed by others . . . can only result in driving a wedge between the white and colored people of Mississippi and will in a short time destroy the peace, harmony, good will and understanding that has existed between the white and colored people of Mississippi for so many years. I do not believe that any loyal Mississippian, white or colored, who has the welfare of his family and our great state at heart, will sympathize with the action by this one Negro with the assistance of the NAACP." Governor Coleman, as already noted, took this action as an incentive to press again for a new state constitution or, at the least, for a new set of voting laws.

After a series of legal maneuvers in which the state tried to have the indictment quashed and Darby attempted to enlarge the scope of his suit, the case went before a three-judge federal court in July. It was brought out at the trial that the number of Negro voters in Jefferson Davis County was down from 1200 in 1955 to a figure Circuit Clerk Daniel put at between 45 and 50. However, Daniel declared that Darby was denied the right to vote solely on the basis of the tests administered to him under the provisions of the 1954 constitutional amendment on voting requirements, and offered several examples of Darby's written answers as proof that Darby was in truth not qualified to vote. Among these were the following:

Darby's interpretation of Section 123 of the state constitution which says "The Governor shall see that the laws are faithfully executed" was interpreted as "the govenner govends all the works of the state and he is to see that all voilatores be punished and als he can pardon out the penetenter ane pherson."

In writing his understanding of the duties and obligations of citizenship under a constitutional form of government, he wrote that "a citizen is persn has been in the USA all his days, and is not been convicted of enny crimes and has been Loyal. to his country and pase all his tax."

133

On November 6 the Court handed down its decision upholding the constitutionality of Mississippi's voter registration laws and rejecting the contention of Darby and Ruth Dillon, who joined Darby in the suit after it had been heard, that they had been denied the vote because they were Negroes. Citing the illiteracy and near-illegibility of Darby's written answers, the Court said:

> We are unable to find any tangible proof that any white person was treated in any manner more favorably than plaintiffs or any other Negroes. The mere showing that of 3,000 qualified voters in Jefferson Davis County only 40 or 50 are Negroes is not sufficient. The disparity between numbers of registrants, as has been so often pointed out, results doubtless from the fact that one race had a start of several centuries over the other in the slow and laborious struggle toward literacy.

The Court further commended Daniel for doing "a hard job in an honorable way" and said the NAACP could appeal directly to the Supreme Court if it desired. Medgar Evers indicated that the case would be brought before the Civil Rights Commission instead.

The Citizens' Council, in commenting editorially on the decision in its November issue, raised the question as to why the nation's press and networks had not covered the story as fully as they would have if the decision had gone in favor of Darby and the NAACP. It noted:

> Besides, we cannot conceive of any mis-named "liberal" editor in the North with guts enough to risk the wrath

of assorted alphabetical minority groups by conceding the simple fact that there exists in the South not just one, but several Negroes incapable of demonstrating the simplest command of written and spoken English.

What is it these one-way liberals fear? Have they so little confidence in their ability to brainwash their people that they are terrified at the thought that a grain of fact might sprout among their weeds of vilification and propaganda? Or is their fear the one shared by all forces of evil in the face of the power and might of a dedicated people, armed with zeal and clothed in the raiment of truth?

In the same issue that carried the story on the Court's action, *The Citizens' Council* renewed its attack on the NAACP. Under a cartoon entitled "The Mau Maus Are Coming," the paper carried the following article.

A brief collection of related facts:

Ebony is a magazine published by Negroes for Negroes.

Medgar Evers is a Mississippi Negro, the state's field secretary for the NAACP.

The November issue of *Ebony* contains an article by Medgar Evers, "Why I Live In Mississippi."

Some quotes from that article:

"He reads extensively of Jomo Kenyatta's Mau Mau reign of terror in Africa, and dreamed of arming his band of blackshirts and extracting an 'eye for an eye' from whites who mistreated his black brothers.

". . . his dream of an American Mau Mau band, roaming the Delta in search of blood.

"I'll be damned if I'm going to let the white man lick me."

Out of context as these quotes might be, they were the kind of statements by a Negro which would most anger and infuriate white Mississippians and many non-Southern whites as well, and the kind which *The Citizens' Council* had proven itself most capable of exploiting. In fact, the most obvious aspect of Citizens' Council activity since 1955 in respect to the Negro was that initiated and carried on by its propaganda agencies such as its newspaper and through its home office in Greenwood. With the exception of Clennon King's abortive attempt to register at the University of Mississippi there had been no school integration efforts or serious threats of attempts since 1955, and this absence of organized Negro activity had much to do with the slackening of economic intimidation and physical violence. As *The Citizens' Council* of February 1957 put it:

In this connection it may be remembered that less than two years ago all was not peaceful in Mississippi as it now is. Then our state was in the midst of an infamous and highly exploited case. . . . With patient organization and education, peace and good order were finally restored in our state. . . . Mississippi, it might be added, has not had one single school suit, or bus suit, and all is peaceful and serene with regard to race relations.

The abatement of violence in the period 1956–58 was offset by the steady intensification of the other kind of activity aimed at the Negro, or rather at the white Mississippian's concept of the Negro, illustrated by the printing of Medgar Evers' statements in *Ebony* in the Council newspaper. An early example of this activity came to public attention in September 1955 when two segregationists played to a crowd in Hoxie, Arkansas, what they claimed was a recording of a speech given by an Arkansas member of the NAACP to a meeting of Negroes in Jackson, Mississippi. The men had obtained the record, they said, from the Mississippi Citizens' Council after conferring with Robert Patterson and Senator Eastland a few days earlier in Mississippi. The record itself was well designed to infuriate the white audience. The "NAACP" man "told" his audience that the ultimate goal of all Negroes should be intermarriage, and assured the gathering that the glorious day was not far off.

There was no more mention of this record until the latter half of 1956, though it was used extensively in Mississippi. At that time, however, certain areas of the South were swamped with mimeographed texts of a speech purportedly by "Professor Roosevelt Williams" of Howard University before a NAACP meeting in Jackson. In the "speech," very similar to the one played in Hoxie, the "professor" "told" his audience that white women had a secret yen for Negro men, and that it would be no trouble

137

at all for any Negro to have sexual relations with anyone he chose.

Attorney General Cook of Georgia apparently had enough faith in the "text" to have it distributed in the official envelopes of the State Law Department, and this led to its ultimate exposure as a hoax. The editor of the Columbus, Georgia, *Ledger-Enquirer* made a thorough check and came up with the fact that there was no such professor as Roosevelt Williams at Howard. He then printed a lengthy editorial stating this fact and calling upon the attorney general to repudiate the whole thing.

On September 5 Cook did publicly disclaim responsibility for the distribution of the text and gave his own explanation of how he had come across it in the first place. He had received the text, he said, from the Mississippi Association of Citizens' Councils. When he phoned Robert Patterson to repeat the charges made by the *Ledger-Enquirer*, Patterson said that "we never claimed it to be authentic." Patterson added that the speech had allegedly been made at a small Negro church, "somewhere in South Mississippi," shortly before the Arkansas elections two years before, but that "it is up to them [the NAACP] to prove it is not authentic."

This was the most important instance of the Citizens' Council being called publicly on some of its material and forced to back down; but there were many other instances of inflammatory anti-Negro or anti-NAACP literature being put out by the Council. A case in point is an editorial which ran in the June 1956 issue of *The Citizens' Council*. It said:

According to the newspapers, the Supreme Court has evaluated Southern womanhood at 10¢ per lady. That is the price any colored man can pay for the right to sit next to a white lady on a bus.

You pays your fare and you takes your choice. What do the "moderates" propose to do about this latest legalized atrocity?

There was much more of this "scare" writing in *The Citizens' Council* through the following year. Some sample headlines which indicate this included: "Crime Mags Protect Wanted Negro Criminals," "Army Covering Up Negro Crime Rate with Double Talk," "40% of NAACP Leaders Linked to 'Red Front' Groups," "Drive for Equality Hatched in Moscow," "Fund for Which 'Republic'?," "Mixed Love for Negroes and Whites," and "Mixer's Aim Is Intermarriage."

The letters to the editor which were included in *The Citizens' Council* were usually extremely rabid. Long stories of "atrocities" committed by "uppity" Negroes were poured out by indignant ladies in at least three issues of the paper while the call to arms was sounded constantly by other correspondents. One wrote:

Of course he and they [the Southerners apathetic to the racial crisis] will wake up some day; just in time to see some sloe-eyed, pigeon-toed Red, and a blue gum Detroit black, come up and take his car and his bottle . . . and, perhaps, his wife and daughters. Then the dumb cluck will holler: "why hadn't somebody warned me?"

The Council also printed and distributed a number of single-sheet handouts designed to show the Negroes' overwhelming desire for integration and intermarriage, or to prove the Negro's basic inferiority. Handouts of the latter type were printed under such titles as "Crime Report Reveals Menace of Integration," "The St. Louis Story—Integrated Schools Hurting Both White, Colored Pupils," "The Ugly Truth about the NAACP," and "Mixed Schools and Mixed Blood."

To many Southerners such material is highly inflammatory, but the Citizens' Council would take no responsibility for any resulting violence whatsoever. In an editorial in the January 1957 issue of *The Citizens' Council*, Simmons wrote:

> Did the Citizens' Councils bring about the present intolerable conditions in Birmingham, Montgomery, Mobile and Tallahassee? Of course not! Did the NAACP? The Urban League? The Southern Regional Council? The Ford Fund for the Republic? Dozens of Communist front organizations? The United States Supreme Court? The question has only to be asked for the answer to be obvious. The responsibility for any violence lies squarely upon those who would compel an entire people to violate their finest instincts.

The sorry examples of what this violation of a people's "finest instincts" had supposedly brought the North in juvenile delinquency and race troubles were heavily exploited in *The Citizens' Council*. In commenting on the publicized suggestion of a blind white girl to President

Eisenhower that the way to end racial intolerance was to blindfold everyone, thereby shutting out all the unimportant distinctions between peoples, *The Citizens' Council* said: "If life were only so simple. The method suggested by Leah [the blind girl] didn't work for the 13-year-old Brooklyn schoolgirl who is so nearly blind she cannot identify the two Negro boys in her integrated school who raped and beat her." The lead story for that issue was "Violence Grips Integrated Schools."

In a later editorial, "Power of Self-Destruction," in the June 1958 edition, William Simmons wrote:

> It is race contact that produces a race problem. But only racial integration can reduce a nation to impotence and decay. The battle to prevent racial integration can be won, but only if white men and women in every village, every city, every state put aside all other considerations—be they political or economic—and through their combined strength preserve the racial integrity of America.

The methods used by the Council to produce that "combined strength" among the white men and women of Mississippi required as much effort and organization as those directed at the Negro. In the following chapter the "battle to prevent racial integration" will be examined from the perspective of its effect on the white community.

CHAPTER V

The Citizens' Councils and Conformity in the White Community

There are scalawags among us today just as there were in Reconstruction days—people who live among us and thrive upon us, but who are willing to sell us out to the mongrelizers. Integrationists who live among us are much more dangerous to our cause than those who live in New York or Illinois.

Robert B. Patterson, *Fourth Annual Report,* July 1958

THE ORIGINAL ATTITUDE of the Citizens' Council toward whites who disagreed with its position on racial matters was first outlined by Arthur Clark, as noted earlier, when he declared that all "right-thinking" Mississippians should join in the battle against a considerable part of the leadership in the Protestant and Catholic churches, large segments of the press, and those "so-called" liberals. He further stated that "the medium of economic pressure can be used quite effectively to the end that those who stir up discontent may be removed from the community." This demand for total white conformity has been preserved to the present day.

Numerous indications are apparent. Perhaps the best illustrations come from the pages of *The Citizens' Council,* which more than anything or anyone else speaks officially for the Citizens' Council in Mississippi. One issue carried a reprint from the Prentiss, Mississippi, *Highlight* which said:

> Are you a member of the Citizens' Council? If you are not, Join Today. . . . The time has come when there is no middle ground. . . . You are either for or against the vital question facing the South and the Nation.

In the same issue, William Simmons wrote:

> Fence straddlers condemning Council members as "extremists" are nothing more than spiritual comrades of Revolutionary War "moderates" who doubtless regarded Paul Revere as an extremist and hate monger. . . . There have always been such "moderates" on hand to decry active resistance to injustice.

The Jackson *Daily News* was quoted in *The Citizens' Council* as saying:

> Common sense calls for a solid front . . . We are up against enemies who would destroy our way of life and

put an end to the traditions so precious to our people. An impregnable front is absolutely necessary.

One other editorial from *The Citizens' Council* emphasized the feeling of the Councils when it said:

Few can doubt that we are facing a juggernaut. Only another juggernaut can cope with it successfully. The materials are at hand, so let us about our work systematically and methodically. With clear minds and sure hearts, let's build it.

Judge Brady expressed the same point of view, though in slightly different terms, when he stated in an interview in February 1957:

Certainly I know that there are plenty of sincere people who are against integration and yet who do not believe in our organization. However, to meet an organized enemy you have to be organized, and there is no room for doubt on that score.

It was not by spoken intentions alone that the Council made its opinion evident in this regard. In the period 1954–58 there were a number of recorded instances of direct Citizens' Council action to insure that a "juggernaut" would be created from the raw material of the white citizens of Mississippi.

The first instance of the Council's uncompromising attitude toward any break in the conformity of the white community came when a baseball game between a touring Negro team and a white team was scheduled in Greenville in September 1954. The Negro team had played white teams in other Mississippi and Southern ball parks without incident; but on Saturday before the Sunday game was to be played, anonymous handbills were scattered over Greenville from an airplane asking, "Are You Proud of Greenville?" and promising the city economic retaliation if the game was not cancelled. A group of men identifying themselves as members of the county Citizens' Council then threatened to hold a sit-down strike in the middle of the diamond if the game was held. The all-white board of directors of the Greenville ball park refused to reconsider its approval of the game, but the promoter decided that the bad publicity would not make it worth his while and substituted two Negro teams instead. The Citizens' Council emerged having made its point, and no game with "mixed" participants was played in the Delta thereafter.

The Greenville *Delta Democrat-Times* protested against this pressure in vigorous terms; and during the rest of the year it periodically attacked the Council for actions taken by some of its members. Then, on March 7, 1955, an article written by the *Democrat-Times* editor, Hodding Carter, appeared in *Look* under the title, "A Wave of Terror Threatens the South." The article reviewed the previous course taken by the Council and gave some of the author's predictions on the movement's future. While the Council was not shown in a favorable light, the effect was considerably heightened by the magazine editor's choice of title and accompanying pictures (one of which depicted a Negro and white child playing together, and another a burning cross surrounded by Klansmen).

On April 1, 1955, the House of Representatives of Mississippi, by a vote of 89–19, censured Carter for lying about the state and the activities of the Councils, and for "selling out the state for Yankee gold." Among the 19 who voted against the resolution of censure was Representative Joel Blass of Stone County, the leader in the fight against the constitutional amendment passed on December 21, 1954. In a speech during the debate on the resolution of censure, Blass said that, as far as he knew, everything in the article was true and added, "I have already felt the lash of the Citizens' Councils . . . It [the article] is the truth as I know it." He went on to describe the methods the Councils had used to discredit him in the constitutional fight, one of them being a circular which listed him, Carter, and Oliver Emmerich of the McComb *Enterprise-Journal* as being linked with the NAACP in their opposition to the amendment.

The day after the censure, Carter wrote an editorial suggesting that all those who had voted for the resolution of censure "go to hell and wait there for me to back down" and implying that the main reason the resolution had been passed was that the Council had a voting membership of 60,000 while he had only one vote. Certain members of the Council then began approaching Greenville merchants, identifying themselves as Council members, and warning the merchants that unless they discontinued advertising in the *Delta Democrat-Times* they would lose all Citizens' Council members' business. Several of the merchants did temporarily cut down on their advertising and some subscriptions were canceled, particularly in the rural areas, but over-all the paper suffered little sustained loss. For the next three years, in fact, Carter's paper was to keep up a constant stream of criticism of the Council and in turn was subject to continuing attacks by *The Citizens' Council* and the various local and state Council officials. In the case of the *Delta Democrat-Times* and its editor, unlike some others, the paper's reiterated support of public school segregation in Mississippi, combined with its position in the community, helped to blunt the effect of the Council's efforts.

There were other targets in Mississippi's white community for the Citizens' Council, however, that were far more vulnerable to attack than the *Delta Democrat-Times* or its editor. The first notice for several of these future targets came with the libel suit brought in late 1954 by the Holmes County sheriff against Mrs. Hazel Brannon Smith, the editor and publisher of the Lexington, Mississippi, *Advertiser* and Durant *News,* both weekly newspapers. Mrs. Smith was found guilty by the county jury of writing a "false" account of the shooting of a Negro by the sheriff and ordered to pay him $10,000. One of the witnesses for the defense in that trial, Dr. David Minter, later recalled the campaign which was waged against those who testified in Mrs. Smith's behalf. He wrote that "as part of the pretrial campaign to discredit Mrs. Smith and also to discredit me as a witness, there were many rumors spread all over the county that I was a Communist, that I was heading a spy ring and holding secret meetings, that I was distributing Communist literature . . ."

The findings of the jury were stingingly reversed by

the State Supreme Court, but apparently some of the charges and the whispered smears made during the trial stuck in the minds of many Holmes County natives. At any rate, less than a year later Dr. Minter had to face much the same charges, but this time in a far different "court."

The first story of his prolonged ordeal appeared on September 29, 1955, in a United Press story from Tchula, Mississippi, a small community also in Holmes County. It said:

A crowd of 700 white men and women crammed into a high school gymnasium Tuesday night adopted a resolution expressing the community's "opinion" that Dr. D. R. Minter and A. E. Cox, cooperative farm manager, should move from this heavily Negro-populated area.

Cox was the manager of the Providence Cooperative Farm where Minter lived and ran a low-cost clinic whose patients were mostly Negroes. Both were Southern-born and educated. Holmes countians had long been suspicious of the activities of the two men, feeling vaguely that they were "socialistic," but until now there had been no direct action taken against them. At the mass meeting they were both accused of fostering "certain practices" which were contrary to the laws and mores of the state. Specifically, they were accused of promoting interracial swimming on their farm and of conducting mixed classes in which they advocated integration. Both men explicitly denied all the charges and suggested that an investiga-

149

tion be made. The unruly crowd ignored both the denial and the request, and instead relied upon a tape-recorded interview by the sheriff with a pair of Negro boys in which the boys stated that such practices did go on at the farm.

The next day United Press reporter John Herbers filed a story which began:

> A widely publicized mass meeting in which two white men were invited to leave Holmes County for allegedly teaching racial integration was held under the auspices of the pro-segregation White Citizens' Councils, reliable sources said today.

> The meeting was called by leaders of the Citizens' Councils in Holmes County and advertised by word of mouth as a council meeting. . . .

> William Moses, a local businessman, is head of the county chapter. County Attorney Pat Barrett is head of the Lexington chapter, and State Representative-elect J. T. Love is head of the Tchula chapter.

All three of the men were at the meeting, Herbers went on, and Love had instigated the call. Minter wrote of this aspect of the "trial":

> There is very little which can be definitely blamed on the councils or rather the organized efforts of the councils . . . it is hard to say if the council would have bothered about us if the sheriff had not laid the groundwork, although eventually there would have been something done because of our opposition to them (not open but just the fact that we did not join). . . . Al-

though no one admitted that the CC planned the meeting, it was certainly through their organization that word spread; also, at the meeting that night one prominent man from Goodman recommended that a committee be appointed to investigate and report to the councils!

As for the results of the trial, he continued:

Most planters stopped sending patients to me; there were a few exceptions, but there was evidently a concerted effort on the part of council members to boycott me . . . One former [white] patient confided in me while drinking that he would have been to see me but that the council had told them to stay away . . . There was no real boycott as far as service went; people still sold us gas, brought supplies to the grocery, extended credit as always. The thing that the council did was to let loose "the winds of fear" . . .

The combination of elements which finally drove the men out of the state are too complex to go into here, but certainly the most important consideration for both of them was the feeling that their usefulness on the cooperative farm was ended and that they would be a liability to any Negroes in the community they might try to help. Definitely they did not "run away."

The ramifications of the meeting did not end with the two men being driven out of the community. At the "trial" a handful of men had tried to face down the crowd. Among these was the Reverend Marsh Calloway, a Presbyterian minister from the nearby Holmes County town of Durant, Mississippi, and a personal friend of Minter and Cox, who publicly termed the meeting "undemocratic" and questioned the moral and legal ethics of using the tape recording as evidence. Eight days later, by the unanimous vote of the elders of his church, he was asked to resign from his pulpit. A spokesman for the elders said that the remarks made by Reverend Calloway caused many of the church's 60 members to "lose faith" in the minister. "His usefulness is at an end here," the spokesman said.

In a letter that Reverend Calloway wrote soon after being dismissed, he spoke of the hysteria which was being bred in the state as "frightening" when it could even come to the point that he, a convinced segregationist, should be dismissed for defending two white men as "good Christians."

The elimination of Minter and Cox apparently opened the way for a concentrated effort to force Mrs. Smith out of business. Alabama-born and a Mississippi newspaperwoman for 22 years, all of them spent in Holmes County, she had often incurred enmity for her crusades against gambling and bootlegging in the county, Mississippi being a "dry" state, but by and large had not touched often editorially on the race issue. After the libel trial and the subsequent reversal of the decision, however, her old enemies started spreading the word through the county that she was an integrationist and even worse.

In the course of the next three years a number of methods were used to spread this portrayal of Mrs. Smith, most of them through Citizens' Council members. Her "sins of omission," as she has described them, were heavily exploited. These included her refusal to attack President Eisenhower's use of troops in Little Rock and to praise Governor Faubus' behavior in the same situation; refusal to attack Governor Coleman's "moderation"; and the major failure of refusing to belong to or go along with the policies of the local Citizens' Council, which had been one of the first organized in the state.

Those interested in silencing Mrs. Smith took advantage of several happenings which, considering the climate of opinion in Mississippi at the time, were windfalls in their attempts to label her as an "integrationist." Among these was her acceptance of an American Traditions Award given in 1957 by the Fund for the Republic. To understand the local implications of this it must be remembered that *The Citizens' Council* had labeled the Fund a Communist-infiltrated organization dedicated to immediate integration.

Particularly untimely and unlucky for Mrs. Smith was another event in the same year. A Negro magazine, *Ebony*, obtained, without Mrs. Smith's knowledge or consent, a picture of her from *Time* magazine and proceeded to run it in a story about the brave Southern women who were fighting for integration. Her picture was carried, moreover, despite the fact that she was not mentioned in the article and is, in point of fact, a segregationist who rarely lets a column on the racial question go by without reaffirming that she is one. Nevertheless, the *Ebony* story was immediately picked up by the group opposing her and circulated throughout the county. On a state-wide level Mrs. Sara McCorkle, a leading Citizens' Council official and paid organizer, used copies of the issue on her tours of the state's high schools to illustrate her set speeches on "integrationists within Mississippi."

The immediate result was that Mrs. Smith lost a good many of her advertisers, and it seemed certain that she could not continue to publish her paper. A letter from *Time* explaining the matter, which she promptly printed, helped ease the situation somewhat. Then her friends in Holmes County came to her aid and many of those who had at first been shocked by the article came around to the realization that Mrs. Smith was not actually the integrationist portrayed. Her paper continued publication with the sole casualty being her husband, who lost his job as manager of the county hospital because he was too "controversial."

The circulation and advertising of her paper steadily declined over the next year and a half, but seemingly the decline was not fast enough. Mrs. Smith's enemies brought their ultimate weapon into play against her in the first week of December 1958. In a meeting attended by some 35 businessmen and farmers, $15,000 was raised toward an anticipated $30,000 to start a new paper in Lexington to compete with the *Advertiser*. Present at the meeting, as at the mass meeting which "convicted" Minter and Cox, were Wilburn Hooker, state representative, founder of the Holmes County Citizens' Council and a member of the State Executive Committee; County Attorney Pat Barrett, William Moses, State Senator T. M. Williams and former State Representative Edwin White. At the conclusion of the meeting Moses said, "This is not against anybody. This is just to get a paper with an editor that thinks like we do. This paper will not take sides in controversial issues."

The man chosen to edit the paper, and the one responsible for most of the early publicity surrounding its formation, was Chester Marshall, Mrs. Smith's general manager for the past year, a fact which provoked Mrs. Smith to comment that "the thirty pieces of silver have become thirty thousand dollars by today's inflation." Marshall stated that, contrary to printed reports, the paper would have a definite editorial policy and that he would be the one who controlled it. He also announced that the new paper would begin operation early in 1959, as it did.

Mrs. Smith wrote in her paper in the same month:

Freedom of the press is again under attack in Holmes County. A new newspaper is reportedly being organized by some group which they say does not like the editorial policy of the Lexington *Advertiser*. . . .

Today we live in fear in Holmes County and in Mississippi. It hangs like a dark cloud over us, dominating every facet of public and private life. . . . None speaks freely without being afraid of being misunderstood. Almost every man and woman is afraid to try to do anything to promote good will and harmony between the races . . . afraid he or she will be taken as a mixer, as an integrationist or worse . . . if there is anything worse by Southern standards. . . . I am not an integrationist, have not been and never expect to be . . .

155

This is not a lone woman editor you are fighting, it is not just a newspaper . . . it is an institution interwoven into your life and the life of the community and county. It recorded . . . your triumphs and sorrows, the good and the evil for 121 years. . . . And it will still be around to carry your obituary.

As of January 1959, many of Mrs. Smith's good friends thought that it was none too certain that these were more than brave words. The opposition of the Citizens' Council by itself seemed sufficient to many to defeat Mrs. Smith in the long run even without the establishment of a new paper. As one of her friends put it:

The Citizens' Council can raise plenty of money to put a moderate out of business. The NAACP can raise money to do what they want to do. But the moderates aren't organized and they seem to have no way to help each other. It's a sad thing, and every time one of them is silenced it makes the others less willing to speak out and do anything. I personally think Hazel's paper is on the way out and I hate to see it, but what can you do?

In Jackson on January 5, 1959, William Simmons refused to see the Holmes County newspaper fight as a Council matter at all. He said to a visiting college student that as far as he was concerned there was "no connection whatsoever between the local or state Citizens' Council and the newspaper in Lexington. The paper started on the initiative of the leading businessmen in Lexington, and the largest element is one of local competition."

In another part of the state a strident and direct attack upon the Councils was and had long been made by P. D. East, the editor of *The Petal Paper*, a tiny weekly in the small town of Petal in Southern Mississippi. An admitted opponent of segregation, East's approach to any problem is the straight lunge for the throat, and it is characteristic of him that he would turn vociferously upon the Council when it organized in his home county. In his column, "East Side," he wrote on March 15, 1956:

Like prostitution, bigotry and intolerance must be a high profit business—else there wouldn't be so much of it.

I am curious to know which minister is going to bless the organizational meeting of the Citizens' Clan next Thursday night.

Forrest County has 12,000 Negroes, all citizens of the United States, but their citizenship expires at 7:30 P.M. next Thursday [the night the Citizens' Council was to form].

Were it within my power to do so, I would not deny the right of organization to the Citizens' Clan. They are within their rights to form . . . but they are not within their rights to use economic pressure as a force against those who disagree with them. They are not within their rights to interpret the laws of the United States, or to subject their own views in religion.

From that point on, according to East, he became subject to general economic pressure and was forced to cut his paper to a four-page tabloid in March of 1957 because he could no longer sell enough advertising to support a larger edition. Considering the fact that he has not made any attempt to hide his opposition to segregation, it would seem that no organized boycott was necessary to deprive him of most of his local readers and advertisers. East himself says that he does not know positively that the Citizens' Council was responsible for his economic plight.

East had and has one factor working for him that Mrs. Smith did not. As vehement critic of all his region's mores, and as a very effective though heavy-handed satirist, he draws attention and subscriptions from all over the nation. In fact, by January of 1959 he was able to boast in *Harper's Magazine* that his paper had the lowest circulation in its home community of any in the world that still could continue publishing, thanks primarily to out-of-state readers and advertisers.

Most local Citizens' Council officials make no comment on East at all, although one did give as his opinion that East "belonged in Whitfield," the state mental institution; certainly to many who were afraid to voice their own similar opinions within the state, East stood as a sort of beacon in the wilderness, flailing with complete abandon at all those features of Mississippi life which most bothered them also. The presence of any sort of boycott seemed to leave him untouched.

While it was hard for individual non-conformists to pinpoint the Council as the source of their trouble, Council activity in another sphere drew a large measure of publicity and comment. This activity revolved around the boycott of national concerns' products in retaliation for their "unfriendly" policies in relation to Southern mores or sensibilities, and was brought to public attention in a series of articles in the *Wall Street Journal* in March of 1956.

The first boycott of this sort had its origins in a story published in October 1955 in *The White Sentinel*, a racist newsletter published in St. Louis, which said that Falstaff Brewing Corporation had purchased a life membership in the NAACP for one of its Negro salesmen. The article suggested that the best way any white man could show his displeasure at this action was by refusing to buy Falstaff beer.

The Citizens' Council in Mississippi picked up the story and distributed copies of *The White Sentinel* throughout the state. There was an appreciable drop in Falstaff sales, and John Hamilton, the editor of *The White Sentinel*, gave the Citizens' Council much of the credit for the decline.

The decline must have been alarming because, according to the *Wall Street Journal*, "at the height of the controversy, Falstaff Brewing Corporation flew a vice-president to Jackson, Mississippi, to explain publicly the company's position—and to confer with officials of the segregationist Citizens' Council." The Falstaff official also came with a check in his pocket for $50,000, so related Judge Brady, to "buy off" the alleged Council boycott. The executive committee rejected the check and disclaimed all responsibility for the boycott, but suggested that perhaps a public statement disavowing any support for the NAACP might do much to calm the situation. Falstaff Corporation followed this suggestion and the boycott began to lift, with much crowing from John Hamilton in St. Louis.

Brady insisted that the boycott was purely an individual matter, as did Simmons in a later interview when he said:

If you try to organize a boycott, you create sympathy for the object of such a boycott immediately. As for Falstaff, Ford, Philip Morris, that was more a case of poor public relations on their part, what with Ed Sullivan on that Mercury show always showing mixed entertainment and remarking on the Negro's wonderful personalities, and Falstaff getting that life membership in the NAACP. You just can't expect individuals to buy products when their distributors are obviously doing things you don't like.

Simmons' comment on Philip Morris and Ford had reference to charges that the Citizens' Council took part in boycotts against those concerns and Philco Corporation, after *The White Sentinel* had attacked them for various "integregationist" activities. The Council in Mississippi never publicly endorsed these proposals, but in the March issue of *The Citizens' Council* it was noted that Philip Morris sales had dropped 17 per cent in 1955. The article also said that "Some observers believe recent sales losses may be due in part to this fact, especially in the Southern states. . . ." "This fact" was the support of the Urban

League, the "State Department of the NAACP," which was later violently attacked by *The Citizens' Council*.

The Council, in fact, specifically denied having anything to do with any of the boycotts then or later, as noted by the article in the *Wall Street Journal*. Judge Brady has insisted that the Citizens' Council does not organize or encourage boycotts. As he put it in one interview:

> There has never been any organized boycott that I know of. It is a terrible thing to use and it can cut and hurt deep. But it is interesting to note how the unions and the NAACP protest when they've been using the same weapon for years.

However, the *Journal* continued, while "the Citizens' Councils and allied groups spearheading the battle against school integration disclaim any official policy of bringing economic pressure against businesses . . . it is clear that some Citizens' Councils serve, at the very least, as transmission agencies for information needed for 'spontaneous boycotts.'"

Certainly this "transmission agency" approach was used effectively in January 1958. In that month's issue of *The Citizens' Council* the front-page lead story was headlined "Grandpa's World Book Exposed." The article began:

> The way books are used as propaganda tools to fool otherwise alert American lovers of liberty is well illustrated by the World Book Encyclopedia—a standard reference work in virtually every Southern library, and in the homes of unsuspecting Southern parents . . .

The paper then carried a number of examples of how the encyclopedia was stacked against the Southern way of life. Among the items that shocked the writer, probably William Simmons, were the following:

Scientists group the peoples of the world into three great divisions: Caucasian, Mongoloid, Negroid. The term Negro is used loosely to mean a member of the Negroid group. But no sharp line can be drawn between these so-called races. . . . Negroid physical traits are also found among other racial groups.

Nearly three full pages of the "N" volume are devoted to the Negro written by Ambrose Caliver, a professional agitator for Negro education who used to be the specialist in higher education of Negroes in the U. S. Office of Education. The entire tone of the article is that of glorifying the Negro.

Of race relations, the integrationist-toned article says of the Southern position: "Race prejudice (which is the constant term for segregation) is often simply a form of economic prejudice. It is as much a problem for the psychologist . . . as for the anthropologists . . ." Thus the South's historic belief in segregation is simply mass emotional illness.

This kind of publicity for their encyclopedia did not seem to appeal to the publishers of the World Book. In any case, their Mississippi attorney went immediately to Jackson to find out if the Council could be appeased. *The Citizens' Council* carried the results of the ensuing conference in its next issue. The publishers had agreed to submit the articles mentioned in the January issue of *The Citizens' Council* to a review by a panel of critics who would view them from the Southern point of view. Furthermore, the next issue of the 1958 edition of the World Book Encyclopedia was to contain a reference article on the Citizens' Councils. The World Book was subsequently never mentioned in *The Citizens' Council,* unlike other institutions and individuals with whom the Council found occasion to disagree.

Concerning some of these other institutions, Simmons said in an interview on February 4, 1957:

> Without some degree of military discipline, it would be hopeless to oppose an enemy, no matter how distasteful such discipline might be to you. So it is with us as in war. You can't meet a severe and mortal threat without organizing. The state government is limited to the legislative and political field, which is the least dangerous of all. As a matter of fact, most of the state leaders are with us. But as a state government, it is particularly helpless in the whole fight because it can't be effective in the battle in the fields of *Education* and *Religion* [emphasis by author].

The Council was very active from its inception in filling these voids left by the state government. To indicate how the Councils' members were to fill one of them, the first *Annual Report* of the Council said:

> The Citizens' Councils think and plan as a group and they are able to act as individuals within their various

churches, schools, and any other organizations to which they belong. This has already proved effective in various church denominations in Mississippi.

Whether the Council, either as a group or through its individual members, was responsible or not, several Mississippi churches and church groups had acted as early as the fall of 1954 to dissociate themselves from the stand on desegregation taken by their national church councils. The first ones to do so were located in the two counties which had been the first to organize Citizens' Councils. On November 26 the Methodist Church in Lexington went on record as opposing the support of the Methodist Council of Bishops for the union of the two racially separated divisions of the Methodist Church in the South. On December 1 the Methodist Church of Indianola took similar action. During November the Presbyterian Synod of Mississippi rejected its general assembly's memorial to open its churches and schools to Negroes, and by a vote of 62–40 asked the assembly to "reconsider and rescind such action." A handful of ministers at this meeting spoke against the rejection, but none did so from the position of a convinced integrationist. The Citizens' Council shortly thereafter published a transcript of a speech in defense of segregation given by the Reverend G. T. Gillespie at the synod meeting under the title "A Christian View on Segregation."

A temporary reversal of the trend came when the Mississippi Diocese of the Episcopalian Church released a "Statement of Principle" which was a general call for support of the Supreme Court and eventual integration, but which was not followed up by the church in any way. This counter-trend continued when on April 26, 1955, the Women's Society of Christian Service of the Methodist Church reaffirmed the racial policies of the Council of Bishops by refusing, by a vote of 129–62, to reconsider endorsing that position. The ladies perhaps were inspired by the Reverend Dan Whitsett of Sylacauga, Alabama, who branded the Citizens' Councils "barriers to good race relations in the South" and called upon his audience to stand firm behind the bishops.

Two months later, however, the Mississippi Conference of the Methodist Church met in Jackson and went on record as supporting the continuation of racially segregated church jurisdictions in the state. Thereafter no state-wide body of any church was to register approval of racial desegregation in any form whatsoever.

The reasons for this are easy enough to find. The largest Protestant denomination in the state is Baptist, whose ministers are answerable directly to their congregations. Since in Mississippi most white adults feel strongly that racial separation should be maintained, those few ministers who did not agree with their congregations apparently felt it more expedient not to say so publicly or often. The same general analysis could be made of all the other Protestant denominations, whether the ministers are responsible to their congregations, as are the Presbyterians, or to their bishops, as are the Episcopalians and Methodists.

For those who did feel that integration should come,

the steps chosen to share this belief with their congregation were slow and careful. As one minister put it, "I try to preach logic and racial tolerance wherever possible without directly advocating any concrete steps toward integration." Certainly this was the nearest any Protestant could come toward advocating integration from the pulpit in the period 1954–58 if he expected to retain his usefulness.

The Roman Catholic Church, although committed to integration, did not advocate integration in its parochial schools in Mississippi, nor did its priests often exhort their congregations on the subject of segregation. In fact, clergymen of all faiths were generally silent.

One incident which limned the feeling in the state about the mixing of religion and support of desegregation occurred in the spring of 1956. Upon being informed by an outraged state legislator of the facts in the matter, the University of Mississippi canceled an invitation to the Reverend Alvin Kershaw to speak on "Church Music" during its Religious Emphasis Week. The Reverend Mr. Kershaw had made the mistake, from most white Mississippians' point of view, of announcing shortly before his scheduled visit that he intended to give part of his $32,000 winnings from his appearances on the TV show, "the $64,000 Question," to the NAACP. After the university's action, all the ministers within Mississippi who were also scheduled to speak during the Religious Emphasis Week canceled their appearances and the planned program fell through.

The immediate result of the ensuing uproar was the establishment of a permanent screening commission to insure that all speakers appearing on Mississippi's state-run campuses would express opinions acceptable to most white Mississippians. The other result, and one which any would-be dissenter among the state's ministers was sure to feel, was the steady barrage of articles and cartoons which *The Citizens' Council* carried thereafter on "Red-tinged" churchmen. A sample issue concerned with this phase of segregation's defense had a lead article head-lined "Southern Churches Urge Mixing" and sub-headed "Integrationist Literature Eyed by Southern Baptists." Other articles were entitled "Reds Increase Influence in Many U.S. Churches" and "[Presbyterian] Assembly Condemns Tradition" [i.e., segregation].

The cartoons on the front page of the same issue depicted a goateed, bereted bebop-like figure sitting on a mass of fluff labeled "Cloud 7" and thinking "Integration, Social Gospel, Collectivism." In subsequent issues the social gospel minister was always to be so portrayed, and in at least one other issue, that of December 1958, the Citizens' Council was to pay very close attention to the activities of the various denominations in regard to the promotion of integration, with titles such as "Atlanta Preachers Urge Surrender" and "Catholic Bishops Called Partners in 'Crime against the South.'"

When most state Baptist organizations came in late 1958 to the defense of defeated United States Represent-ative Brooks Hays, the lay leader of the Southern Baptists, groups of Baptist laymen in several Southern states in-cluding Mississippi withdrew from their state organizations and fired off telegrams urging Hays to resign. Similarly, a few Mississippi Presbyterian and Methodist churches had withdrawn from their respective church organizations during the past three years in protest against their support of integration.

In so doing they were following the advice of Judge Brady in *Black Monday* when he wrote:

If the Bishops, the Board of Elders, the Deacons, etc., and the powers that be will not clean up their own back yards, then they must be cleaned up for them. Where the church organizations permit it, it can be done from the floor. Committees from the congregation can be formed which, in turn, can advise the governing authorities what is not to be preached and what is not to be done. If it becomes necessary, and this may be classified as heresy, the Independent Christian Churches of America can be organized, which will not embody within their doctrines any communistic or socialistic concept which is contrary to the teachings of Christ.

By the end of 1958, it can safely be said, virtually the only Mississippi ministers who still publicly expressed any viewpoint on segregation were those who supported its continuation. These were the same clergymen who could be found giving the invocation at Citizens' Council rallies or providing the textual substantiation for such printed throwaways as "Is Segregation Unchristian?" a single sheet distributed by the Council containing a long list of biblical quotes, all but five from the Old Testament, in support of racial segregation. As in other fields, the Citizens' Council or the Citizens' Council viewpoint was uncontested in the state's churches.

Few accusations have been made that the Mississippi Council is similar to the Ku Klux Klan or to some of the Citizens' Councils in other states in having any degree of anti-Semitism or anti-Catholicism in its stated aims or purposes.

Judge Brady had written in *Black Monday:*

It is lamentable that attention should be called to the alarming increase of Jewish names in the ranks of Communist-front organizations of this country. Of all the nations which have ever been on this earth, the United States of America has been the kindest to the Jew. Here he has suffered but little ostracization—and he has brought most of this upon himself . . . From the Jewish race there should never be any Rosenbergs, Greenglasses or Alger Hisses. The Socialist and Communist infiltrated labor organizations should not have the Dubinskys, the Emspals, the Abram Flaxes and Ben Golds as their leaders. . . .

But, he added:

Because of the mistakes of a few of their leaders, let us not condemn a race. Because Arthur Spingarn is President of the NAACP it does not follow that all Jews approve of this rabid organization. . . . Let us remember the loyal American Jew is not responsible for Karl Marx. . . .

The only overt action which smacked of anti-Semitism was the mailing by Robert Patterson of the list of recommended reading in 1954 which contained some anti-Semitic works. This, as noted in the first chapter, gave rise to charges of "anti-Semitism" from some quarters, particularly the Anti-Defamation League of B'nai B'rith, which related that while the Councils themselves might not be expressly anti-Semitic, many of the Citizens' Council members were.

To counter this, the Citizens' Council published a pamphlet entitled *A Jewish View on Segregation*, purportedly written by a Mississippi Jew. The publisher's note says:

This article is entirely voluntary by a Jewish Southerner who prefers to remain anonymous for the simple reason that the people who will agree with what he has to say, or be tolerant of it, will remain silent; the cranks and crackpots who will wish to revile him for his right to form his own beliefs and act upon them will not remain silent.

The most important section of this pamphlet, which is a defense of segregation, is contained in the following paragraph:

But, some have said, the Citizens' Councils are anti-Semitic. Nothing of the sort. Where prominent Jewish leaders have enrolled as members and taken an active part in the duties of the Council, there is no chance of anti-Semitism creeping in. There are communities

170

where Jewish leaders have flatly refused to join, although in these same communities prominent Catholic and Protestant men have joined, despite the stands taken on segregation nationally by their church groups. Who can blame them for feeling a bit bitter against white Southerners who try to stay "neutral" on such an issue. . . . So the Jew who attempts to be neutral is much like the ostrich. And he has no right to be surprised or amazed when the target he so readily presents is fired upon.

When asked about anti-Semitism in the Council in Mississippi, Simmons said:

The Council is definitely not anti-Semitic or anti-Catholic, since we so obviously have members from both groups. You've seen our pamphlet on *A Jew Looks At Segregation*. Well, we sent copies of that to the National Jewish Congress to see what they'd say to it. We didn't get any answer.

If you ask me, if there were no anti-Semitism, some of those Jewish money raising outfits would manufacture it out of whole cloth. It would make about as much sense for us to be anti-Semitic as to be anti-snow in Alaska. It has nothing to do with our problem.

For that matter, Methodists have had more to do with promoting integration than have Jews, and there is even a Baptist on the board of the NAACP.

If there is any pressure against the Jewish section of the white community by the Citizens' Council, it seems to be of a type more implicit in any such an organization than explicit in its stated program, because in none of the state Councils' charters has the phrase "white, Christian" membership or "believers in the divinity of Jesus Christ" appeared, as it has in Citizens' Council charters elsewhere.

One reason the Councils do not move against the Jewish citizens of Mississippi is that in many cases they do, in truth, share the Councils' views. Another is that while a latent anti-Semitism may exist in the white Christian community, it is not strong enough to make its positive expression worth while unless there should be some indication that the Jewish members of the community were going to question Southern racial attitudes. Few Southern Jews have openly done so. Accordingly, they are accepted as conforming members of the white community and not subjects for outright Council discipline.

Indeed, John Kasper, the notorious anti-Semite and leader of the Seaboard White Citizens' Council, wrote to Phillip Luce, a collegiate recruit supposedly, and bitterly denounced the Mississippi Citizens' Council for not engaging in anti-Semitic activities. He wrote:

As you may know, the Mississippi Ass'n of Citizens' Councils does not believe the jew has anything in particular to do with the present scope and direction of the communist conspiracy. I think they know better, but for political reasons, fear of economic reprisals (probably mortgaged to the hilt to jews personally) and red-newspaper smear, they refrain from approaching this great problem. In view of the long-established facts, this is dishonest and amounts to contempt for the people of Mississippi.

. . . I have no doubt that Patterson is sincerely doing what he thinks best and is ardently defending the Southern "way of life" as a segregationist. However, whether through obtuseness or cowardice, Patterson is not telling Mississippians all they should know if he is suppressing, either through ignorance or fear, the facts concerning the jewish peril."

Nevertheless, some influential Mississippi Jews have reported receiving hints from Citizens' Council members that "for the good of relations" between Jews and Gentiles in Mississippi it might be wise for Mississippi's Jews to disavow B'nai B'rith and other national Jewish organizations supporting integration. In some communities a handful of Mississippi Jews have sought to lead such a bolt from the national organizations to avoid "rocking the boat," but thus far such efforts have been unsuccessful. The rabbis, who, by and large, do believe and teach tolerance far more forthrightly than their Christian counterparts, have had enough influence or control so far to block them.

The Citizens' Council role, by the spring of 1957, was unquestioned publicly by any meaningful segment of the adult white community. The Council then took the next logical step and began a bid for a similar conformity and acceptance among the white youth. Several halting moves in this direction had been made between 1954 and

1956. Pro-segregation textbooks were placed in some schools, and one or two high school assemblies were treated to a Citizens' Council speaker; but the full-scale effort was not inaugurated until February 1957. In the issue of *The Citizens' Council* for that month Simmons wrote:

> With this issue we begin the publication in serial form of "A Manual for Southerners." Lest our friends in other sections of the country feel that we are becoming too ardent "Confederates," let us hasten to say that we are not. The truth is that for too long Southern children have been "progressively educated" to scorn their origins and the reason for our bi-racial society.
>
> "A Manual for Southerners" seeks to correct this.
>
> The portion appearing in this issue is for use in grades 3 and 4. However, there are many adults who might benefit from a review of these fundamental truths.
>
> Excerpts from the *Manual* follow:
>
> God put the white people off by themselves. He put the yellow, red and black people by themselves. God wanted the white people to live alone. And He wanted the colored people to live alone. That is why He put them off by themselves.
>
> Do you know what part of our country you live in? You live in the South. You know you live in Mississippi. Mississippi is a state in the South. The South is a big part of our country.

174

Negroes and white people do not go to the same places together. We live in different parts of town. And we are kind to each other. This is called our Southern Way of Life. We do not mix our races. But we are kind to each other.

Do you know that some people in our country want the Negroes to live with the white people? These people want us to be unhappy. They say we must go to school together. They say we must swim together and use the bathrooms together. We do not want to do these things.

"Why do some people want us to live together?" you will ask. They want to make our country weak. If we are not happy, our strong and free country will grow weak. Did you know our country will grow weak if we mix our races? It will.

The *Manual* was continued in the March issue, this time for grades 5 and 6. Two excerpts follow:

Did you know that your great grandfathers did so much to make a free country for you to grow up in and be happy in? No other part of the U.S. is more American than the South. Southerners have always protected the things that are American with all their might.

One thing that made the Americans so mad at England was her terrible idea of slaves. English merchants wanted to make money. They bought Negro slaves from Negro masters in Africa and brought them to America to sell them. The Americans said, "We do not want black men in our country. They will not be happy among white people, and we will not be happy among them." But King George wanted his merchants to make money. So the Americans were made to buy the Negro slaves.

The June issue related:

. . . [after the Civil War] the Negroes moved off to themselves and the white people did the same thing. Both races want to live alone. They feel strange living around each other, because they are different. Of course, the Race Mixers wanted to make the races live right together. They wanted the races to go to the same schools, sit together in the buses and movies, use the same swimming pools and rest rooms together and dance together. These people who want the races to live together have always wanted to cause trouble.

The remainder of the *Manual* is in similar vein. Simmons said in January 1959 that many school principals had requested copies of the complete *Manual for Southerners* and that copies had been donated to a number of school libraries by local Citizens' Councils. The response, he said, had been "quite gratifying."

To enlarge this new approach, the Citizens' Council State Executive Committee announced in January 1958 the appointment of Mrs. Sara McCorkle of Grenada as women's activities director for the state. Soon thereafter Mrs. McCorkle began appearing at numerous women and civic club luncheons. Her principal job, as she explained it to one reporter, was to acquaint high school students with "the necessity of keeping our white race white." In one television appearance she pointed out that some high school students were apparently confused over pro-integration policies that they read of in newspapers and magazines, and that in talks to the students she tried to "point out what has happened to nations that have experienced racial amalgamations."

She continued that "the superintendents have shown wonderful co-operation. Some of them haven't had a chapel program to fit in with my traveling schedule and have called a special student meeting for my talk."

The McCorkle circuit was not the only means the Citizens' Councils employed to reach school-age children. In the late spring of 1958 several local Citizens' Councils sponsored essay contests for high school students, entitled "Why I Believe in Segregation." Then, in September of the same year, *The Citizens' Council* announced a statewide essay contest, offering two $500 prizes for the graduating boy and girl who wrote the best essay on one of four topics. These were: "Why I Believe in Social Separation of the Races of Mankind"; "Subversion in Racial Unrest"; "Why The Preservation of States' Rights Is Important to Every American"; and "Why Separate Schools Should Be Maintained for the White and Negro Races."

Mrs. McCorkle, who directed the contests, said that they had as a threefold purpose: (1) to "assist our young people to develop into informed, patriotic American citizens;

(2) to stress the importance of maintaining States' Rights and constitutional government; and (3) to stress the necessity of maintaining racial integrity." The prize money was to come from the educational fund and May 1, 1959, was set as the deadline. In addition to the two grand prizes, $50 was set aside for each local high school winner.

The Citizens' Council did not confine its attention to secondary school education. Institutions of higher education in Mississippi also needed to conform.

Judge Brady had written in *Black Monday:*

> Unless the true facts involved in these issues [segregation and communism] are placed before the youth of our country, we are doomed. A child does not depart from the way in which he is brought up, and the responsibility of this rests squarely not only upon the shoulders of this country, but also upon the shoulders of the parents of these children. If the educators will not teach these facts, they should be forced to teach them.

In Mississippi some educators did indicate that they were being forced to teach what they did not believe. The Kershaw incident, during Religious Emphasis Week in the spring term of 1956, and the determination to screen all speakers on the state's campuses were apparently the final straws for a few of the professors at Ole Miss. In 1956, the chairman of the University of Mississippi's Sociology Department joined another professor at Mississippi State College in issuing resignation statements denouncing the "intellectual strait-jacketing" in the state's

178

colleges. Both men were promptly censured by the State Senate. Twenty top-level faculty members resigned soon thereafter from Ole Miss during the summer of 1956, and 11 more followed them the next summer. "I'm going to a better paying job in an atmosphere more congenial to higher education," said Dr. Harris G. Warren, a history professor at Ole Miss for 11 years. "I'm tired of the attitude in this state toward higher education."

The harassed chancellor of the university publicly declared that the resignations were the result of low professorial salaries. But some departing teachers angrily disputed this explanation. Dr. Charles Biggers, a philosophy professor, said: "In spite of what the administration says, there is a lack of academic freedom at Ole Miss." He cited examples of efforts to have the library shelves purged of all books about Negroes, and added that the "supersensitive militancy toward the race question poses a very real threat to the scholastic reputation of the University."

The professors at Ole Miss were also upset over the intimidating circulation by the Citizens' Council of a document, signed by Law School Dean Robert Farley, urging respect for the Supreme Court's decision. Although Dean Farley was only one among many eminent lawyers and teachers who signed the resolution, his name alone was circled with a dark black line. Furthermore, it was common knowledge on the Ole Miss campus that a number of students and at least one university staff member kept black lists of those who weren't "right" on the segregation question. These black lists were mailed to the offenders' home-town Citizens' Council organizations. Because of this "atmosphere of intimidation," one departing professor said, not only were good teachers leaving but it was becoming almost impossible to get good replacements for those who did.

Ole Miss and Mississippi State were not the only colleges affected. The most violent controversy of all, and the one in which the Citizens' Council played the principal public role, arose at Millsaps College, a small, high-ranked Methodist liberal arts institution in Jackson. As part of a month-long program sponsored in March 1958 by the Christian Council, an organization of the student leaders of the various campus religious bodies, three lectures on "both sides" of the segregation issue were scheduled. A story which appeared in the Jackson *Daily News* on March 4 quoted the initial speaker, Dr. Ernst Borinski, as saying that segregation "violates Christian premises . . . and democratic principles." Dr. Borinski, a professor at Tougaloo, a privately supported Negro college on the outskirts of Jackson, was reported to have said also to an audience of 16 students:

The Supreme Law of our land cannot be challenged, state laws notwithstanding. [The Mississippi Negro] . . . is not satisfied and looks toward the National Association of Colored People as the legal avenue to get what he wants. He wants to ride the bus in the seat he chooses, go to the schools which are best and go to the shows where the best shows are shown.

The next day the *Daily News* published a story about the second speaker scheduled to present the integrationist point of view. He was to be the Reverend Glenn Smiley, field secretary for the Fellowship of Reconciliation of Nyack, New York. The story quoted William Simmons, the editor of *The Citizens' Council*, as saying: "We feel the public and particularly parents of the students would be interested in being informed of the kind of organization whose employee is to take part in the forum underway at Millsaps." The Fellowship of Reconciliation, he said, was dedicated to promoting integration through "civil disobedience," and listed as its secretary-emeritus A. J. Muste, a "former national chairman of the Workers Party of the U.S.," which "was founded on the . . . principles of the revolutionary theory and practice stated by Marx and Lenin." The *Daily News* then tied in this story with another story concerning a legislative plan to investigate the state NAACP, of which Dr. Borinski was a member.

More fuel was added the next day when the *Daily News* reported an "integrated meeting" at Tougaloo with white sociology students from Millsaps participating in a discussion on race relations with Tougaloo's Negro students. The *Daily News* failed to mention that the classroom was segregated, with the white students on one side of the aisle and the Negroes on the other. Nor was there any indication that this meeting was not related to the lecture series at Millsaps, but a part of a long-range program set up by a sociology professor at Millsaps. A number of Negro and white students were quoted in the article, with the clear implication that the two groups found no basic differences between themselves on most racial matters.

Although Millsaps' director of religious life, the Reverend Norman Bergmark, had canceled the second pro-integration speech the preceding day because it "had been singled out for special notice," this cancellation was not noted by the *Daily News* until the next day. On March 7 the *News* then carried on page eight, after front-paging the story up to that point, the explanation by Dr. George Maddox, the sociology professor at Millsaps, that the Tougaloo meeting had not been a part of the Christian Council series and that "segregated seating was observed." "The meeting was not designated to challenge anyone but was what seemed to me to be a legitimate intellectual pursuit, having nothing to do with my own views of integration or segregation." He said that the newspaper accounts had taken all of the students' remarks out of context.

On March 9, Ellis Wright, probably Mississippi's leading funeral director and the president of the Jackson Citizens' Council, issued a letter to the press which he had simultaneously dispatched to Millsaps College President Dr. H. E. Finger. The letter said that he was "appalled and shocked" by the Borinski talk. "The public is entitled to know . . . exactly what position our administration takes with respect to providing a cloak of prestige and respectability for the furtherance of racial integration. . . . It is intolerable for Millsaps College, right here in the heart of Mississippi, to be in the apparent position of undermining everything we are fighting for. . . . The time has come for a showdown. Either you and your faculty are for segregation or you are for integration. . . ."

The next day Dr. Finger answered Wright's letter. His reply in its entirety follows:

I trust my statement in yesterday's paper will help to interpret to our friends in the community the situation that has troubled us. As the President of Millsaps College I am answerable directly only to the Board of Trustees of Millsaps. This position I hope you will appreciate.

Two of the state's newspapers came to Millsaps' defense during the same week. The Greenville *Delta Democrat-Times* editorially commented that Ellis Wright, "the undertaker who is president of the Jackson Citizens' Council apparently is prepared to embalm and bury the remains of academic freedom in Mississippi. . . . Neither Pope Pius XII . . . the Rabbis of Judaism nor most of the ministers of the established Protestant denominations could pass this Jackson thought embalmer's muster." The Jackson *State-Times* declared that, while the scheduled speakers had not been chosen wisely, the subsequent furor raised by the Citizens' Council had injured race relations. It further noted that "the public evidences extremely little confidence in any position if it is afraid to hear the other side."

Speaking to a student-faculty assembly on March 11, Dr. Finger asserted once more that he was answerable only to the Millsaps Board of Trustees and added, "The real question is not segregation or desegregation, but freedom of speech. Deeper than that, it is who is running Millsaps College and who is running the Methodist Church."

On March 14 Ellis Wright demanded a public statement from the Board of Trustees, asserting that "your failure to make a clear statement of policy will be interpreted as supporting racial integration. . . . A great many irrelevant remarks have been made concerning academic freedom and freedom of speech. No one has the slightest question about these matters. But the public . . . wants to know the answer to one simple question. Where does the administration stand on segregation?"

The Board of Trustees answered Wright with a statement, the next week, which ended the controversy as far as the college was concerned, although it did not satisfy the Citizens' Council. The statement said in part:

> We follow the founders of Millsaps in encouragement of academic freedom in the faculty and the spirit of inquiry in the students. . . . The purpose of a college is not to tell people what to think but to teach them how to think . . . neither segregation nor integration is an issue at Millsaps College. Segregation always has been, and is now, the policy of Millsaps College. There is no thought, purpose, or intention on the part of those in charge of its affairs to change this policy.

> The administration of these principles is the responsibility of the president, and for their implementation he is responsible to the Board of Trustees. The board commends the manner in which Dr. Finger has fulfilled this responsibility.

In the March issue of *The Citizens' Council*, Simmons ran a long editorial headed "College Officials Won't Take

Stand," which outlined the chain of events through the board's statement, and asked:

> Should a society allow its students to be indoctrinated with a viewpoint subversive to its own way of life? This issue is being decided at Jackson, Mississippi, in a controversy between Millsaps College . . . and its alumni, contributors, and community. . . .

> The reader may decide for himself, by reading the text below, whether the trustees came to grips with real issue . . . it is certain that many Mississippians remain acutely conscious of the climate of opinion on the Millsaps campus.

A short time after the Board's statement, Jackson attorney John Satterfield, a prominent Citizens' Council member, presented "the other side" with a pro-segregation speech at Millsaps. This was the last public notice given this matter, primarily because Millsaps is a church-supported school and was therefore beyond the control and retaliation of the state legislature.

As a sidelight to the Millsaps story, the First Methodist Church of Durant, in Holmes County, found it necessary to cancel a scheduled revival because the visiting minister had congratulated Millsaps for "letting young people have an opportunity to hear both sides" of the question. "That's why I support the school and that's why I sent my daughter there," he said. The church sent the minister, the Reverend J. Noel Hinson of Sardis, Mississippi, this letter:

The revival meeting which was to begin next week, March 17, has been cancelled by the official board of this church. Our members had anticipated an inspirational revival with you as guest preacher. However, your letter to Dr. Finger, President of Millsaps College, approving the program of Racial Relations disagreed so completely with our belief in Christian ideals and principles we feel that it is best to cancel your engagement for this revival.

The issue spilled over from Millsaps to Mississippi State College where the editor of the college paper, L. E. Miller, wrote editorially that any school had a right to hear both sides of the racial issue and that the Citizens' Council had been in error. In the next issue he printed a number of letters to the editor, pro and con, including the misspellings.

Miller's printing of one uncorrected letter, with his own "sics" and editorial asides, enraged some students and alumni as much as had his original editorial. In response to the opposition, the Student Council fired Miller from his post. Miller promptly demanded a vote of the student body as to whether or not he should be retained as editor, such a procedure being incorporated in the student body constitution. Though the Student Council's action was upheld by a majority of the students by a vote of 1150 to 950, the vote fell short of the two thirds necessary to sustain his ouster. Miller returned to his job, but not to his editorializing.

Although this was the last publicized incident on a Mississippi college campus arising from the segregation-integration controversy, *The Citizens' Council* devoted a good part of its August 1958 issue to an attack on the National Student Association. The publication referred to the NSA as being Red-front dominated, and characterized its members as being those who were too undesirable for fraternity membership or too sissyfied to make an athletic team. The reason for this attack apparently lay in the NSA's endorsement of integration and its support for the NAACP.

The spring of 1957 had witnessed the beginning of another Citizens' Council project which was far more ambitious than the indoctrination of a few Mississippi school children or collegians. On April 29 the Citizens' Council initiated a weekly television series from Jackson called the "Citizens' Council Forum." William Simmons, writing in the May issue of *The Citizens' Council* said that the weekly 15-minute telecasts were "intended to acquaint the public with the serious problems affecting states' rights and race relations, and with steps being taken to meet them." The first guest speakers were the president and treasurer of the Jackson Citizens' Council. The program was actually the outgrowth of a previous Citizens' Council venture into the mass media which had consisted of one-minute spot advertisements using both films and live appearances.

During the next year the "Forum's" scope was steadily enlarged, with taped broadcasts of its proceedings being made available to a number of the state's radio stations. Then, in June 1958, Simmons announced in *The Citizens' Council* that thereafter the "Citizens' Council Forum" would be filmed and taped in Washington, D.C., and would include public figures from all over the nation. "In the very near future," Simmons wrote, "we anticipate that 'Citizens' Council Forum' can be seen or heard in every Southern home with a television or radio receiver."

By December 1958, *The Citizens' Council* made the claim that the "Citizens' Council Forum," billed as the "American point of view with a Southern accent," could be seen or heard in Alabama, Arkansas, Louisiana, Mississippi, Tennessee, Florida, Texas, Georgia, Virginia, North and South Carolina, and Washington, D.C., and carried a program listing which included some 80 stations. The "Forum" was offered as a free "public service presentation" to any station that asked for it, the financing coming from the dues of Citizens' Council members and whatever extra contributions the Council could obtain. The Council attempted to spur the latter by announcing that they could be considered tax-deductible since they were going to a non-profit organization.

According to one Council official, the cost of producing the programs was about $4000 a month, with the expenses of distribution sure to raise that sum. Certainly, the only factor which might brake a more rapid expansion of the "Citizens' Council Forum's" audience was the matter of finances, but this was a doubtful deterrent. The Council was confident that by the end of 1959 the "Forum" would be presented on a number of non-Southern stations, an indication that in the field of mass communication the organization had been as successful as in that of regional organization.

While to most observers it seemed obvious by mid-1957 that the opposition to the Citizens' Council in Mississippi was at best weak and unorganized, the Little Rock School crisis provided the impetus for a fresh attack by the Council on all those who espoused in any way the course of "moderation." After the first outraged cries in *The Citizens' Council* had subsided, there followed a steady stream of material designed to keep as many Mississippians as possible at fever pitch. The January 1958 issue of *The Citizens' Council* carried an advertisement for a "Remember Little Rock" stamp for two dollars. The design showed a soldier prodding a bayonet at the backs of two white girls. In the same issue appeared, inevitably, a cartoon of a man, "The Positive Thinker," with a brief case labeled "Moderation" and an umbrella "Appeasement."

In April the Jackson Citizens' Council ran a "freedom of choice" survey of all white residents of Jackson. *The Citizens' Council* sub-headed the story "Finds Strong Sentiment against Race-Mixing." The story reported that "Every white resident of the Jackson metropolitan area is due to be contacted by a member of the Jackson Citizens' Council during the course of a block by block survey now being conducted."

Among the questions asked were these:

Do you intend to allow your children or grandchildren to be integrated? (99 per cent said no.)

If you have no children or grandchildren in school, would you support morally and through the Citizens'

Council your neighbors, whose children are the targets of attempted integration? (96 per cent said yes.)

In an emergency, will you cooperate with local Citizens' Council leadership chosen by you and your neighbors in advance? (99 per cent said yes.)

According to Simmons, similar surveys were also begun in Greenwood and McComb, and "interest has been expressed in such a project by Council groups in Louisiana, Florida, Georgia, and North Carolina." He prophesied that "this project will focus attention on the issue more thoroughly than anything else."

The final tabulation of the Jackson survey disclosed, unsurprisingly, that 98 per cent of the white population supported school segregation and promised to support the Citizens' Council in any crisis, according to figures released by the Citizens' Council.

Simmons commented in an editorial in the April *Citizens' Council,* "Vote of Confidence":

Another gratifying response reflects the unanimous public recognition of the ability of the Council's clear-thinking, level-headed leadership to meet the emergency, should one arise. The survey shows 99 per cent of Jackson's white residents will look to the Council for guidance if trouble comes.

Has any other grass-roots movement ever registered a 99 per cent vote of public confidence? We know of none. . . .

This is the highest endorsement the Council movement could receive. It is proof of the essential intelligence of our southern citizens. They have not been misled by wild propaganda claims, nor have the prophets of doom made them fearful.

They know what they want. They are determined. And they are aware that the only way their principle can prevail is through a courageous, united stand.

Misguided counselors of do-nothing "moderation" to the contrary, they want to do something. And they have chosen the Citizens' Council as the instrument by which their high aims can best be accomplished.

There has yet been devised no workable substitute for organization.

The attack on those who did not or would not take an uncompromising stand on the segregation crises continued in *The Citizens' Council.* In the October 1958 issue under an editorial entitled "The Carpetbaggers Are Coming," Simmons described the attitude of the Citizens' Council and any "decent Southerner" toward any Mississippi citizen who would consent to be a member of a state advisory group to the federal Civil Rights Commission.

No decent or responsible citizen in the South will be so stupid as to allow himself to be used for the betrayal of his own people, or so callous as to be insensible to the ostracism that will inevitably follow. Any so called "advisory group" that is eventually scraped from the bottom of the Deep South barrel, we may be sure, will be fit companions of the inter-racial rabble with whom they will associate themselves.

As of January 1959, the Civil Rights Commission was unable to announce any members of its Mississippi Advisory Group, although it had done so in other Southern states.

The defeat of United States Representative Brooks Hays of Arkansas in November 1958, a moderate on racial matters, was happily played up in the November issue of *The Citizens' Council*. A cartoon depicting a dead figure labeled "Moderation," crushed by a ballot box, appeared on the editorial page. Under the heading "Sic Semper Moderation" Simmons wrote:

> We suspect that the advocates of appeasement, of surrender-in-advance which has been mis-named moderation, will remember this election for many a year. . . . Meantime the moderates in the South are consigned to oblivion. They have gone the way of the Whigs, while emitting the bellows of a Bull Moose in the process. May their tribe decrease!

Attacks on moderates and moderation were not confined to the pages of *The Citizens' Council*. With a gubernatorial election slated for the summer of 1959, most of those making candidate-like noises were also busy denouncing moderation. These candidates saved their most bitter diatribes for Citizens' Council audiences.

Ross Barnett, a veteran though hitherto unsuccessful gubernatorial campaigner, told the Wilkinson County Citizens' Council that the Councils were the reason why "we have been able to maintain segregation in all public places in Mississippi." The Councils, he went on, "do not pursue in any manner the avenue of moderation. From my observation, it is not the policy of the Citizens' Councils to sit around and do nothing with sweet thoughts and apathy."

Representative John Bell Williams, who had toyed with and abandoned the idea of running for governor, told the Edwards Citizens' Council on December 5, 1958, that "there is no place for moderation in the fight to maintain racial separation. There are no moderates in the camp of our enemies—they want nothing less from us than unconditional surrender. We face the most vicious kind of extremists in this struggle, and we cannot afford the luxury of moderation, complacency, or timidity."

Judge Brady told an audience in Canton, Mississippi, that a moderate is "a man who is going to let a little sewage under the door."

The end of 1958 was marked by this kind of oratory, with little or no reply from whatever proponents of moderation remained in the state. With the election campaign sure to grow warmer as summer approached, the likelihood was that the attacks on any deviation from total resistance would increase rather than diminish.

That the Citizens' Council of Mississippi could see little to block its future expansion within the state at the close of its first four years of existence seems apparent. As to its future course, only time can actually tell, but there are certain elements of the movement and certain aspects of Mississippi itself which provide some possible clues as to a probable future.

CHAPTER VI

The Future of the Citizens' Councils in Mississippi

We have no other alternative. The choice is between victory and defeat. Defeat means death, the death of Southern culture and our aspirations as an Anglo-Saxon people. With strong leadership and the loyalty and fortitude of a great people, we will climb the heights. Generations of Southerners yet unborn will cherish our memory because they will realize that the fight we now wage will have preserved for them their untainted racial heritage, their culture, and the institutions of the Anglo-Saxon race. We of the South have seen the tides rise before. We know what it is to fight. We will carry the fight to victory.

Senator James O. Eastland, 1955

The Citizens' Councils are not just a pro-segregation movement. They represent the substantial beginnings of a fundamental conservative revolt. The thousands of men who have given unstintingly of their time and substance are moved by a deep unrest that has been growing for the past 25 years. . . .

The Citizens' Councils are not just a sectional, Southern movement. It is significant, to name one instance, that we find ourselves working side by side with other patriotic groups in the North, to defend the Walter-McCarran Immigration Act from heavy attack by the Communists and their allies.

The Citizens' Councils, as you have seen, are not just an extremist minority. They represent the broad stream of thought and attitude of our section.

William Simmons, 1958

THE CITIZENS' COUNCIL as of January 1958, stands virtually unquestioned in its dominance of the white community in Mississippi. Its record to date has been one of impressive successes interrupted only infrequently by temporary setbacks, and there is no readily apparent reason for expecting this course of events to be altered in the immediate future. It has the paid allegiance of possibly 80,000 Mississippi whites and the support of many thousands more. Those actions in which it most openly indulges are approved, for their stated aims, by the great majority of the white population of the state. The Council is, in short, best categorized as an exaggerated but largely accurate symbol of Mississippi's reaction to the threat of desegregation.

The Council's position in Mississippi is made more secure by the fact that its local and state leadership is drawn primarily from the ranks of the white community's business, political, and social leadership. Such men have been in control of the movement in Mississippi since its inception, and because of their guidance no offshoots of the Ku Klux Klan have been established in the state. While certain local organizations have indulged in clandestine activities reminiscent of the old Klan techniques, they have been neither condoned nor sanctioned publicly by the Council's leaders.

The class represented by the Council hierarchy can be seen both in the State Executive Committee and in the local branches. A look at the top four appointed officers of the State Committee is indicative; it should be remembered that the other 24 elected members of the Committee are generally from the same section of Mississippi society. The state treasurer, R. P. Parish, is president of the Bank of Greenwood; William Simmons, state Administrator and editor of *The Citizens' Council,* was a businessman in Jackson before becoming the full-time, assertedly unpaid editor of the paper; Finance Chairman Ellett Lawrence is the owner of a prosperous printing company in Greenwood, made no less prosperous by the printing of most Citizens' Council mailing pieces; and Robert Patterson, the executive secretary, was a planter before devoting himself full time to the segregationist cause.

On a local level the composition of leadership is usually the same. According to William Simmons, the Jackson Citizens' Council board of directors includes "8 lawyers, 2 bank presidents, 3 manufacturers, 1 gas utility president, 1 electric utility executive vice-president, 2 paper company owners, 2 insurance agents, 1 funeral director, 3 house-wives, a deputy state tax collector, a TV station manager, a dentist, 3 public relations men, an investigator for the Public Service Commission, a dry cleaner, 3 union men (AFL, CIO, RR), a supermarket manager, the State Bank Comptroller, an oil man and a general contractor."

In Greenville in 1956 the chairman of the county organization was a bank president, the president of the Greenville Council was the wealthy owner of a barge line, one of the vice-presidents was a city councilman, and another was a doctor. Of the 28 men on the Greenville Citizens' Council board of directors, at least 10 were business owners or managers, two were doctors, three were lawyers, and two held public office. In Clarksdale the Citizens' Council advised any new prospects for membership to "walk into the nearest bank" to sign up.

Judge Brady has insisted on several occasions that prospective Council members are screened before being accepted to insure that "the rabble and the fanatics are kept out." While it is doubtful that such screening is used in many of the local Councils, the firm retention of control in the hands of the more prosperous and conservative members has served to restrain for the present those who favor a policy of more overt intimidation of the Negro and non-conforming white.

Nor does there seem to be much likelihood that this type of control will be threatened in the near future—barring any immediate attempt at school desegregation, an eventuality which will be discussed later. If nothing else will serve to keep the present leaders in power, the mechanism set up for the election of the State Executive Committee should be sufficient to do so. To present this as simply as possible, the Citizens' Councils in the various organized counties, which include all but a few of Mississippi's 82 counties, hold a special meeting once a year and elect county chairmen. The state association is composed of these men, but in practice they delegate their authority to the State Executive Committee. The 24 men on this committee are elected by the Council officials in the state's six congressional districts, four from each district. Thus it would take a full-scale movement among the local officers of each district to unseat or destroy the Executive Committee's control in that district, and with the power of non-recognition as its chief weapon the Committee could excommunicate any local organizations which attempted this.

By giving each congressional district an equal voice, the Council showed a further degree of foresight in heading off any future cry of "area domination" which otherwise might have arisen. Factionalism is an old story in Mississippi, the split between Delta and Hill country being one of the major realities of state politics. A Delta-controlled movement might well have had no success whatsoever in other parts of the state. While three out of the five appointed officers of the State Committee are from the Delta, there is no sign of unhappiness on this account. The Council is in truth a state-wide organization, its only weak area being the Gulf coast with its low percentage of Negroes.

A constant reiteration of "respectability" and "non-violence" has been the main prop of the Council in maintaining its appeal to the middle and upper class strata of the state's white population. It is a theme which has been an integral part of the Council's propaganda since its birth and it has been highly successful. Judge Brady summarized this approach in a speech in Indianola in October 1954, which the Council later reprinted and distributed in pamphlet form. He said:

> . . . And unless we keep and pitch our battle on a high plane, and unless we keep our ranks free from the demagogue, the renegade, the lawless, and the violent, we will be branded as we should be branded, a fearful, underground, lawless organization.

Most local Councils take their cue from the judge's words in this speech rather than from some of his suggestions in *Black Monday*, and in their constitutions and frequently published "objectives" strive to maintain the aura of respectability. A fairly indicative "Declaration of Objectives" was put out by the Greenville Citizens' Council in September 1955. It reads in part:

> That we do reaffirm our faith in and allegiance to the Government of the United States and the Constitution thereof, reserving only the right guaranteed by that Constitution to protest against the usurpation of the power and encroachment on the rights of the Sovereign States to govern themselves; and

> That we do reaffirm our previously announced objectives to maintain separation of the white and colored races in the public schools of Greenville and in all public

places used for amusement, recreation or service of food and drink which have customarily maintained such separation in the past; and

That we do hereby pledge ourselves that in reaching our objective we will use only peaceful and lawful means, reaffirming that strife and violence are foreign to our beliefs as members of this organization. . . .

To emphasize further this attitude, the Mississippi Citizens' Council makes it a standard practice to disown immediately any connection with those segregationists outside the state whose actions become as violent as their words. Thus, despite the fact that Judge Brady had written him a long letter of warm endorsement only a few months earlier, "Ace" Carter, the rabid leader of the North Alabama Citizens' Council and a Ku Klux Klan leader as well, was repudiated instantly by the Mississippi Council when his notoriety threatened the reputation of the Council. In a letter published for general Council consumption in January 1957, Robert Patterson wrote:

In a movement of this size, it is to be expected that certain crackpots, fanatics, and misguided patriots will mistake notoriety for support, and will do and say things that will certainly not express the opinion, or be sanctioned by Council members in general. . . .

Our members know that our Councils have prevented violence, and will continue to do so, here in Mississippi. Integration, with its accompanying frustration, will definitely cause violence in Mississippi or any place else in the South. That is why we organized against integration; to prevent violence.

Concerning another well-publicized segregationist rabble rouser, John Kasper, William Simmons declared:

We're rather suspicious of Kasper, and in fact have been getting some peculiar reports on him. You know, when he was in New York he was a member of one of those anti-Semitic organizations which is financed by Jews as a sort of stalking horse. In fact, we have a feeling he might be a plant. What he is doing is just what I'd hope a Citizens' Council member would do if I were in the opposition.

However, Simmons offered another view on the Council's responsibility for the actions of the more violent segregationists. He said:

Ace Carter is an Alabama problem. He has no standing with our group. We have refrained from poking our nose into their business so that they will always refrain from intruding into ours. We don't seek the headlines, though, but would rather be quiet and peaceful and get the job done.

However, it might be added that the NAACP never feels it necessary to apologize for every Nigger rapist, or for the Commies who help their cause, and I think they play it smart. Start apologizing for something and you admit your association with it.

Apology for any of its activities has never been one of the distinctive features of Council utterances, whereas an aggressive presentation of its point of view whenever and wherever possible certainly has been. A wide variety of reading material is offered for sale at nominal prices by the Council headquarters in Greenwood, the books offered ranging from *Black Monday* to Herman Talmadge's *You and Segregation* to *The Deep South Says Never* by John Barlow Martin. The latter is an amplified version of a series of articles that Martin wrote for *The Saturday Evening Post* on the South-wide Council movement, a series which the Council has warmly endorsed as the best presentation of its viewpoint and history yet attempted. The Council also offers pamphlets by such men as James F. Byrnes, William Simmons, Senator James Eastland, Congressman John Bell Williams, and Georgia Attorney General Eugene Cook. By Simmons' 1958 reckoning the Council has distributed nearly eight million pieces of literature since it was founded in 1954, and reaches an audience of over 150,000 people with its radio and television programs— probably a conservative estimate now. According to Judge Brady, "The Citizens' Council paper has a circulation of 65,000 [in 1958]. It is sent into every state of the union and is placed on the desk of every state legislator and important public official. Every high school library receives it. Every member of Congress and the personnel of many Federal agencies likewise receive this paper."

Further to establish its respectability, the Council's officers have sought and accepted invitations to speak at gatherings outside the South. The race issue and the Council's stand on it are never soft-pedaled by the speakers; but, depending on the audience, there is usually a slanting of the emphasis to fit the situation. Judge Brady, in the middle of a speech in San Francisco to the Commonwealth Club of California on October 4, 1957, which was largely a distillation of *Black Monday,* said:

Primarily the Councils are dedicated to the preservation of segregation and the sovereign rights of the states of this union. They are opposed to the communizing and socializing of our labor organizations, churches and schools. The Citizens' Councils are determined to do everything within their power to prevent the broadening of the power of the Executive branch of our government, and the usurpation by the judiciary of powers vested solely in Congress. They are determined to resist the enormous and unwarranted pressure which is brought to bear on both major political parties and on all branches of our government by the left-wing minority groups. The Councils will resist to the bitter end the proposed welfare state and its destruction of the obligations and liberties of the citizens of this country. Above all, the Councils are dedicated to non-violence and have prevented lynchings and mob action in the South. The Councils firmly believe that within the confines of the true constitution of this government and within the constitution of the respective states, an orderly, peaceful and legal means exist whereby these objectives can be secured and maintained.

Overlooking the "preservation of segregation" as one of Judge Brady's points, this passage could have come from almost any conservative's campaign speech in almost any section of the country. William Simmons hammered out a similar line in a speech to the Oakland, Iowa, Farmers-Merchants Annual Banquet on February 3, 1958, when he said:

Has it occurred to you that the social revolutionaries who are working to remake the South in their own image are not just interested in racial integration? They are above all collectivists. They are driving for increased national power. The South has to be dealt with because it stands squarely in their way as the strongest remaining bulwark of our constitutional form of government that protects your property rights and your personal freedoms as well as ours.

How long do you think that you would enjoy your own rightful interests if these revolutionaries succeed in establishing a totalitarian welfare state in Washington? Do not deceive yourselves. Since 1932 the New Deal, the Fair Deal, and the other Deals have never wavered from one course. However soothing the words or how alluring the promises, that unswerving course is the steady march toward an all powerful centralized government.

Simmons said in a later interview that although the Council did not have any direct legal affiliation with any other group, it did have a day-to-day working arrangement with one or two national organizations. Among those he mentioned were the Daughters of the American Revolution and the American Legion, both usually placed among the more conservative forces in America. The presence of many Council stalwarts in the Federation for Constitutional Government and the States' Rights movement are similar manifestations of this drive among many Council leaders to reach some conservative haven.

Nevertheless, despite the obvious desire of the Council's state leaders to make the Citizens' Council into something more broadly based nationally than merely a pro-segregation movement, and despite the attraction such efforts have had for some of the Council members in Mississippi, the fact still remains that the majority of the Council's members belong to it not because of its "respectability" or its conservative credo, but because it serves as an organized channel for their deep desire and intention to maintain segregation and to freeze the Negro in his present status in Mississippi. All oratory aside, this is the basic drive behind the Citizens' Council in Mississippi and throughout the South.

What is more, as citizens of Little Rock, Arkansas, and Clinton, Tennessee, to name the two most obvious examples, have found, the claims of "non-violence" and "respectability" are discarded soon enough when the chips are down. Simmons himself, while denying the Citizens' Council *at present* condones or encourages violence in Mississippi, said that in this regard "public sentiment is the supreme arbiter." He also said that in the event of integration, or even of Civil Rights legislation which might drive the Citizens' Council underground, "great violence will be inevitable, of a kind to make the present stuff look like child's play. Any violence which has occurred so far has been spasmodic and unorganized, but I could not speak for the future course of events in such a situation."

Actually this is the biggest problem for that section of the Citizens' Council leadership which wishes to continue as a "respectable" organization in the fight to prevent integration. Any wide-scale integration attempts whatsoever, in the immediate future in Mississippi, are sure to bring violence, the state having had four years of incessant oratory that integration will never take place if the battlements were manned in sufficient strength.

If such violence occurs, the Council will have to decide which side of the street to work—that of violence or that of non-violence. If it chooses the former, the movement as it is now constituted would disappear, because a large portion of its members from the upper and middle classes would not stand for such activity under their own auspices, no matter how ardent they might be in the defense of segregation. On the other hand, if it chooses the latter, the Council stands to lose an even larger portion of its membership to whatever rabble rouser comes along to promise a last-ditch fight, with blood in the streets and all the other features that the Council's leaders have promised and warned of so forebodingly in the past.

To this writer, at least, it seems clear that in the event of attempted mass integration "respectability" would go to the wall and the old Ku Klux Klan approach would emerge triumphant. The Council's motto, "Dedicated to the maintenance of peace, good order and domestic tranquility in our community and in our state and to the preservation of our States' Rights," would soon enough boil down to "Segregation at Any Price," and it would be a motto a large minority of white Mississippians would rally around with a vengeance. The sifting off of the more conservative members because of disapproval of the new methods could in time isolate the Council from the rest of the white community, but the trail it might leave before this isolation was completed could well be a bloody one.

This is the blackest picture of the future, however, and one which is not actually expected to materialize. It is more likely that school integration on a secondary or grammar school level will not be attempted for some time, or when attempted will be in a carefully selected community on a piecemeal basis. In this case it is probable that there will be no state-wide bloodshed and violence, and even more probable that whatever violence does occur will be unorganized and spasmodic. Most of the battle would be fought in the courts, and even with some limited integration the Council could come out stronger than ever. Whatever limited integration gains were achieved would be effectively manipulated as symbols for further resistance, and the state would stay firmly in the hands of the "immoderates." There is a perspective other than short range, however; certain factors within and without the state should in the long run serve to undermine the Council's position or nullify its effectiveness in the state.

The first and most obvious factor is that when integration is attempted in Mississippi, it may well be the last major bastion of "massive resistance" in the South. Already Arkansas to the west and Tennessee to the north have areas of at least token integration, and the collapse of Virginia's total segregation structure may well prove to be the decisive event in the struggle between integration and segregation. What is more, unlike the days of Reconstruction, Texas and North Carolina are also missing from the ranks of total defiance.

This is not to suggest that integration would be any more welcome to the mass of white Mississippians later than it is now; but the collapse of regional solidarity would deprive the Citizens' Council of its most telling point in favor of organization and defiance on a massive scale. There are few men anywhere who will wholeheartedly fight to the last ditch in a cause which is already lost, no matter how sincerely they may believe in that cause. The isolation of Mississippi would rob the Council of much of its appeal and vitality. While there would still be strong sentiment for closing the public schools rather than submitting to any integration at all, the failure of such a solution in other states should soon be apparent to most citizens of Mississippi, a state which more than most is dependent upon its public schools for its population's education.

On an even longer range basis, disregarding for the moment any integration attempts, there are certain trends within the state which, if projected, would serve to reduce the appeal or effectiveness of the Citizens' Council. Among these the most important is the gradual reduction in the proportion of Negro to white, at present somewhere around 45–55. The pressure of numbers is a very obvious reason for the perpetuation of many of Mississippi's racial mores, no matter how hard the proponents of immediate integration may try to discount it. Few white Americans have ever lived in a community in which the population of non-whites is, if not larger, equal to that of the whites. Nor have many Americans grown up with a heritage of fear that this large minority or actual majority of the population is patiently awaiting an opportunity to rise up and in one fell swoop exchange its position of inferiority and servitude for one of dominance. Understanding this, it should be easy to understand also why those areas in which the Citizens' Councils have had their greatest organizational success have also been the areas in which Negro density is the highest—particularly the Yazoo-Mississippi Delta.

While the thesis cannot be seriously advanced that a change from a Negro population proportion of 45 per cent, or 60 or 80 per cent as in some counties, to 20 or 15 per cent would be the panacea or the antidote for Mississippi's racial problem, it would eliminate a major source of this problem. What is more, it would eliminate a major support of the Council. Without this pressure of numbers, it would be harder to convince many Mississippians that only organization could stem the "faceless, classless, raceless flood" that Council propaganda plays up so heavily.

Another factor is similarly a long-range one, but in view of the current activities of the federal government in the field of Civil Rights it may not be so distant as the first. This is the matter of Negro voting, which as of January

1959 was at a very low ebb. It is probably true today that because of the poor educational facilities which were offered the Negro in the past, and the lack of incentive or ability to attend those schools that were available, most of Mississippi's Negroes of voting age are at present not qualified to pass even a fairly administered test under the requirements of Mississippi's voting laws. However, with the improved and still improving caliber of education which is being offered him in Mississippi, the Negro will soon be a potent force in Mississippi voting—assuming that upon meeting the requirements of the voting law his right to vote is guaranteed. This assumption is based on the likely further one that either Mississippi on its own initiative, or under the prodding of the federal government and courts, will provide such a guarantee.

When the Negro is reckoned with at the polls in Mississippi, the day of the Council as the dominant force in Mississippi politics will be over. Council officials are well aware of this. Many echo Simmons' declaration on Negro educational possibilities that "There is far too much preoccupation with the myth of education. Education is made to sound like a cure-all, which it is not. We must remember that the ability to reason is not related to the ability to read or write." The right or ability of the Negro ever to have a voice in the governing of the state is constantly challenged by Council leaders, and for good reason. But in this, time would seem to be working against them.

Another possible factor in the future of the Citizens' Council in Mississippi is the gradually improving economic position of the Negro. This is as slow and torturous a process as any mentioned so far, but it will eventually progress to the point that the Negro will not be as open to economic retaliation as he is now. When more Negroes work in factories than on farms or as house servants, when more Negroes live in cities than in rural communities, the most direct or violent forms of pressure will no longer be possible. What is more, the white community may well discover what white communities in other areas where the Negroes' buying power is heavily concentrated have found: that economic retaliation is in truth a two-edged sword. Whatever the case, the diminution of the power of intimidation would go a long way toward stripping the Citizens' Council of its tremendous power within the total structure of Mississippi life.

An improving economy would likewise affect the Citizens' Council's hold upon the white community as well. Certainly an improved economic picture within the state would go a long way toward holding some part of the estimated 75 per cent of Mississippi's college graduates who leave the state for greener pastures. Despite the efforts and claims of the Council, many of Mississippi's college-educated youth do not accept all tenets of the segregationist faith, whether they believe in segregation or not—as most of them do. As more of them remain in Mississippi to assume eventually positions of leadership in their communities, the Citizens' Council will have fewer and fewer recruits from the middle and upper classes. Likewise, most of the new industrial managers from the North who are moving into the state will be apathetic recruits for the Council. Again this will not bring about an immediate withering away of the Council, but it will lower the community standing it now enjoys with all the power that such standing implies.

All other possibilities and conjectures aside, however, the basic factor which will ultimately destroy the Council as a major force in Mississippi and the South is the fact that it is essentially a negative movement, founded on the defense of the status quo and dedicated to its preservation, and dependent on the existence of a similarly negative outlook among the white population. Defense of the status quo, as history has shown often enough, is an arduous task at best. When, in a democracy such as ours, it involves the repression of a minority, it becomes an impossibility.